The Ascending Organization

Upgrade your corporate fabric: How to end the vicious circle of disengagement, disempowerment and stifled innovation.

Copyright

The Ascending Organization

Table of Content

Introduction 7
1. Obsolescence 9
    Soulful Workplaces 9
    Our current blueprint is obsolete 11
    Corporate culture 16
    Definition of the corporate fabric 19
2. Fabric Upgrade 21
    A New Fabric is needed 21
    The proposed fabric 22
    Towards the new fabric 25
3. Personal Awareness 28
    Our Programming 28
    Fear-based behaviors 30
    The Good news 33
    Practical tool-1 38
    Practical tool-2 40
4. Organizational Awareness 43
    Question your structure 44
    Decision making 47
    Accountability and Sensing Tension 49
5. Your Vibration 53
    The Importance of your needs 56
        Nonviolent Management 57
        Nonviolent Communication 101 59
        The art of giving feedback 65
        The even more difficult art of receiving feedback 71
        Towards more productive meetings 75
        From enemy images to empathic inclusion 80

Strengths - Cultivate your Unique Brilliance 84
Dominant vibration 88
6. Performance through agile structures 92
Holacracy 94
The example of Zappos 99
Decision Making Process 101
Distributed Power 104
Accountability 108
Common misconceptions 111
7. Your Leadership 115
Heart-Based Leadership 118
Trust-based Leadership 126
Data confirms what great leaders knew already! 126
The power of trust 128
Characteristics of trust-based leadership 133
How Conflict can be Healthy 135
Mindful interactions in the workplace 136
And then ... performance 139
8. Innovation Unleashed 140
Speed, Agility and Innovation 140
The fertile ground for innovation 144
9. Purpose 150
Being guided by purpose 151
Profits 161
Closing Note 163
About the author 164

Introduction

I have always been amazed by how much we (individuals and companies) take care of our equipment (cars, electronic devices, machines, IT systems, production systems, …) by constantly upgrading and repairing them.

Take your smartphone for instance. Don't you constantly upgrade our phone's operating software ? And for some, even the hardware, the actual device, every year with every new release? And the applications that sit on top of your phone …

But what do we do to keep our human capital alive, rejuvenated, healthy, inspired and engaged? So little. Luckily, the human «machine» is more flexible and adaptable than actual machines. But only to a certain extent…

I strongly believe we need to take a different approach to how we view our workplaces as well as to management and leadership:

- What kind of leadership do we need to reach new levels of performance, which is ecological and sustainable for all parties?
- What can we do to help others feel more motivated and engaged in what they do at work?
- What new type of communication do we need to develop?
- How do we unleash everyone's potential, creativity and innovation?
- What form of organization and governance lead best to innovation, and empowerment?

- How can we contribute to our colleagues' full potential development and growth?
- How can we lead with both the head and the heart?
- How can we reach new levels of performance while not ignoring our whole self at work ?

This calls for a different type of leadership. A radical upgrade …

Just as I was writing this book, I have found myself in situations at work (and heard about others) whereby colleagues ended up crying. Out of anger, fear or despair. As I was reflecting on the reasons why this could even happen, I realized they all led to a number of root causes which could be categorized as either personal or organizational.

This book is therefore about the upgrade (personal and organizational) our corporate fabrics need. It shows that to achieve greater levels of performance and innovation, we all (leaders, managers and coworkers) need to upgrade both ourselves and our organizations' fabrics (culture, decision making, processes, power distribution, mindset, behaviors and accountability level, engagement …)

And as both upgrades go hand in hand, benefiting each other's transformational processes, leading to more soulful and purpose-driven human beings, managers and organizations, new levels of performance are unleashed.

Disclaimer: As you may have noticed by now, English is not my native language. Although I do work (write and speak) in English, I have no doubt you will occasionally find in this book few awkward turns of phrase. Despite a long and thorough review process. I hope you will be forgiving when it does happen.

Chapter 1
Obsolescence

Soulful Workplaces

As a way of introduction, I would like to start with how Frederic Laloux depicts some of the symptoms we encounter in today's workplaces.

Frederic Laloux in his book « Reinventing organizations [1]» researched 12 organizations who fundamentally use new ways to manage work and their employees. These so called evolutionary-teal organizations[2] are self-managing, agile and adaptive, and they deliver extraordinary results.

Here is the picture the author paints in the early chapters of his book :

> *"We are increasingly disillusioned by organizational life. For people who toil away at the bottom of the pyramids, surveys consistently report that work is more often than not dread and drudgery, not passion or purpose. <...> . And it's not only at the bottom of the pyramid. There is a dirty secret I have discovered in the fifteen years I have spent consulting and coaching organizational leaders: life at the top of the pyramids isn't much more fulfilling. Behind the façade and*

---

[1] http://www.reinventingorganizations.com/

[2] http://www.leadershipandchangemagazine.com/reinventing-organizations/

the bravado, the lives of powerful corporate leaders are ones of quiet suffering too. Their frantic activity is often a poor cover up for a deep inner sense of emptiness. The power games, the politics, and the infighting end up taking their toll on everybody. At both the top and bottom, organizations are more often than not playfields for unfulfilling pursuits of our egos, inhospitable to the deeper yearnings of our souls"

"An increasing number of us yearn to create soulful organizations, if only we knew how. Many of us don't need convincing that new types of companies, schools, and hospitals are called for. What we need is faith that it can be done and answers to some very concrete questions. The hierarchical pyramid feels outdated, but what other structure could replace it? How about decision-making? Everybody should make meaningful decisions, not just a few higher-ups, but isn't that just a recipe for chaos? How about promotions and salary increases? Can we find ways to handle such matters without bringing politics to the table? How can we have meetings that are productive and uplifting, where we speak from our hearts and not from our egos? How can we make purpose central to everything we do, and avoid the cynicism that lofty-sounding mission statements often inspire? What we need is not merely some grand vision of a new type of organization. We need concrete answers to dozens of practical questions like these"

"Can we create organizations free of the pathologies that show up all too often in the workplace? Free of politics, bureaucracy, and infighting; free of stress and burnout; free of resignation, resentment, and apathy; free of the posturing at the top and the drudgery at the bottom? Is it possible to

reinvent organizations, to devise a new model that makes work productive, fulfilling, and meaningful? Can we create soulful workplaces—schools, hospitals, businesses, and nonprofits—where our talents can blossom and our callings can be honored?"

Yes, there are companies which have achieved great level of engagement and are known to be great places to work. But the symptoms described here sometimes seem all too familiar, don't they ?
The question I often asked myself is simply "Why" ? Why is our work even source of so much suffering ? If not suffering, disengagement ? Why could the corporate world not be a place of fulfillment ? Of expression ? Creativity ? What does prevent it ? What needs to be changed or transformed ?

Our current blueprint is obsolete

Clearly, if we look at the corporate world today, we can only be saddened by the many issues we face in our organizational lives.

Engagement

According to Gallup, the percentage "engaged" among the U.S. working population has remained at around one-third (currently 33%) since it began measuring it in 2000. And the percentage engaged globally in the 100+ countries where Gallup measures it has hovered around 15%.

Only 13% of employees worldwide are engaged at work, according to Gallup's 142-country study on the State of the Global Workplace. In other words, about one in eight workers -- roughly 180 million employees in the countries studied -- are psychologically committed to their jobs and likely to be making positive contributions to their organizations.

The bulk of employees worldwide -- 63% -- are "not engaged," meaning they lack motivation and are less likely to invest discretionary effort in organizational goals or outcomes. And 24% are "actively disengaged," indicating they are unhappy and unproductive at work and liable to spread negativity to coworkers. In rough numbers, this translates into 900 million not engaged and 340 million actively disengaged workers around the globe.

Those are staggering numbers, and still indicate we have not found the recipe to have our workforce engaged.

Dis-empowerment and Extrinsic drivers

No surprise then, that we find our colleagues to be mostly driven by extrinsic drivers, such as reward and promotion. Needless to say that both matter in the corporate world, but has never been really a sustainable lasting way of being engaged at work. People feel dis-empowered most of the time, and will tend to find excuses for all kind of reasons.

Analysis paralysis and slow decision making - Painful meetings

Who has never been in meetings where there is barely an agenda, no clear outcome and next steps, and no decision being made ?

Meetings are sometimes merely a place where we can express our opinions and agree, or disagree, with what others are saying. It is natural for us all to want to be right as this is gives us a way to feel valued and appreciated. Agreed, not rushing a decision when there may be millions at stake is certainly a "good thing". But when analysis paralysis becomes the norm, when decisions are too slow to be taken, and when people are being driven by fear or by their ego, this has repercussions on the company agility and products or services' time-to-market.

Lack of accountability

This is one of the most visible consequence of disengagement! Lack of accountability. Have you ever noticed that when we are fully engaged in what we do, being accountable comes naturally. Things are flowing, we collaborate, we get things done. As a manager, I have often used in my career quarterly MBO (Management by objectives) with my teams. The definition of each team member's MBO has to be as S.M.A.R.T as possible : Specific, Measurable, Achievable, Realistic and Time Bound. One way I can quickly identify MBO that are not SMART enough is by looking at the verbs used in their definition as I will ask team members to come up first with their own proposals. I have found it to be difficult for many to be able to define SMART MBO. Some would use very vague and generic verbs such as "support", "help", "drive", "participate" …

Whether conscious or not, the use of those verbs , more often than not, would indicate a lack of accountability. Interestingly, when your engaged employees start to use those verbs, this is a very likely indication that you have a culture in which accountability needs to be revisited and looked at.

Ignoring the signs

As a consequence, people start to ignore the signs. When you do not care, when you are disengaged, you are less likely to pay attention to details or feel empowered to remediate specific tensions you sense in your job, or in others. Even worse, some will start to not even care. Those are the things you know needs to be done, or needs to be escalated, but are not being raised. We all have our reasons for it, but this is a bad organizational disease.

Fear

Working in environments where fear prevails is clearly really sad. Workplace should provide joyful and soulful opportunities to express our talents, and yet, we often act out of fear. Fear of being fired, of conflict, of accountability, … The list is endless.

Alignment issues - Politics

"Alignment" and his brother "Misalignment "! Those terms are so often used, mostly to serve as an excuse to delay activities, sometimes until they get forgotten. I am exaggerating, of course, there is always something, someone, which or whom we need to align to. That leads to more slowness and paralysis. You can sometimes work with people that have become such experts at mastering the art of alignment that they end up spending most of their time in meetings and internal politics !

Communication issues

As people are being driven by fear, consumed in internal politics, one immediate collateral damage is the loss of authenticity we can see in personal relationships and communication. We do not communicate with authenticity anymore, we wear masks, we avoid telling what is right and alive in us to instead start to please others. We think that in order to fit in, we need to watch our communication style, we need to comply. Unfortunately, this can lead over time to more disengagement and separation. And poor business performance.

Innovation programs - Change Management programs

Lastly, one word on innovation programs. Throughout my career, I often have been involved in various internal innovation programs. While some were truly successful, and did deliver on the promise of fostering more innovation in certain aspect of the business, the sad reality is that they were exceptions. Same applies to change management programs. While their original objective was to radically challenge and evolve the way we had been doing things, most just ended up being complete failures.

According to various studies from academics or consulting firms, it is said that only 70-80% of innovation programs or change initiatives are doomed to fail. We will discuss later in this book reasons why that is, but why would one expect to be able to reignite a stronger innovation spirit on a soil formed by a disengaged workforce ?

Going through this list, you may have nodded a few times, relating to some, if not all, of the issues discussed above.

Sadly, the collateral damages for us all of going through those challenges are immense.

It creates suffering, disillusion, disengagement and only takes us away from what should be. Which is, workplaces as opportunities for expression of ourselves, our creativity, our talent, our need for connection and contribution and collaboration.

Corporate culture

In this first chapter, I would like to introduce the notion of the corporate fabric, which I see as something more encompassing and broader than the traditional company culture we have known for many years.

But before I do that, let's have a quick look again at what a company culture really is. We like to talk about our culture at work, challenge it, passionately debate it, without always having a clear idea of what it really is !

Much has been said or written on corporate or organizational culture, therefore the definition below can only be a simplification.

In a nutshell, an organizational culture is a system of shared assumptions, values, and beliefs, which governs how people behave in organizations. These shared values have a strong influence on the people in the organization and dictate how they do things in their jobs.

The company culture is the personality of a company. It defines the environment in which employees work. Company culture includes a variety of elements, including work environment, company mission, value, ethics, expectations, and goals.

Corporate culture refers to the beliefs and behaviors that determine how employees interact and handle outside business transactions. Often, corporate culture is implied, not expressly defined, and develops organically over time from the cumulative traits of the people the company hires.

While awareness of corporate or organizational culture in businesses and other organizations such as universities emerged in the 1960s, the term "corporate culture" was developed in the early 1980s and widely known by the 1990s. Corporate culture was used at this time by managers, sociologists and other academics to describe the character of a company, not only through generalized beliefs and behaviors, but also through company-wide value systems, management strategies, employee communication and relations, work environment, attitude …

Just as national cultures can influence and shape a corporate culture, so does a company's management strategy. In top companies of the 21st century, such as Google, Apple Inc. and Netflix Inc., less traditional management strategies that include fostering creativity, collective problem solving, and greater employee freedom have been the norm. It has been argued that this is also the key to these companies' success.

Some recent, high-profile examples of alternative management strategies that significantly affect corporate culture include holacracy (which we will examine in more details later in this book) and the shoe company Zappos, and agile management and the music streaming company Spotify. Holacracy is an open management philosophy that, amongst other traits, eliminates job titles and other such traditional hierarchies. Employees have flexible roles, and self-organization and collaboration is highly valued.

Characteristics of Successful Corporate Cultures

The Harvard Business Review identifies six important characteristics[3] of successful corporate cultures in 2015. First and foremost is "**vision**": from a simple mission statement to a corporate manifesto, a company's vision is a powerful tool. Secondly, "**values**," while a broad concept, embody the mentalities and perspectives necessary to achieve a company's vision.

Similarly, "**practices**" are the tangible methods, guided by ethics, through which a company implements its values. For example, Netflix emphasizes the importance of knowledge-based, high-achieving employees and, as such, Netflix pays its employees at the top of their market salary range, rather than an earn-your-way-to-the-top philosophy. "**People**" come next, with companies employing and recruiting in a way that reflects and enhances their overall culture. Lastly, "**narrative**" and "**place**" are perhaps the most modern characteristics of corporate culture. Having a powerful narrative or origin story, such as that of Steve Jobs and Apple, is important for growth and public image. The "place" of business, such as the city of choice and also office design and architecture, is also one of the most cutting-edge advents in contemporary corporate culture.

Definition of the corporate fabric

Let me now introduce the notion of what I would like to call the "corporate fabric", which just resonates better with me than "culture" while also being broader in scope.

Admittedly, one of the reason it resonates so well with me has very likely to do with the fact that I have worked for many years in the Information Technology sector. Fabric is a term that has been

---

[3] https://hbr.org/2013/05/six-components-of-culture

used heavily in the last decade in IT. So, let me first try to draw on that analogy while trying not to be too technical!

In information technology, fabric is a synonym for the words framework or platform. In general, the term fabric describes the way different parts of something work together to form a single entity. In this context, fabric is used as a metaphor to illustrate the idea that if someone were to document computer components and their relationships on paper, the lines would weave back and forth so densely that the diagram would resemble a woven piece of cloth.

In networking and IT infrastructure, we would define a fabric by looking at several attributes, including:

- the regularity and connectivity of the various nodes
- the design of the traffic flow, specifically how traffic is channeled to individually connected devices
- the performance goals the topology is designed to fulfill in terms of forwarding information

When we have those attributes, we tend to see the whole infrastructure as a single entity, which can deliver certain level of performance in a very predictable manner, the Holy Grail in IT !

We can now look at how to transpose this analogy in the corporate world.

The way I tend to be looking at the corporate fabric is as a superset of our traditional corporate culture. A corporate fabric would be a combination of personal attributes and organizational attributes.

Examples of personal attributes:

Behaviors
Accountability level
Level of engagement
Level of trust
Communication style

<u>Examples of organizational attributes:</u>

Structure
Decision making processes
Flow of Innovation
Authority distribution and delegation

If we go back to the description of a fabric found in IT, I like to look at the corporate fabric as what connects the different parts of the company (organizations, teams, individuals, processes…) , how they are connected and what they create in terms of performance and employee engagement.

Chapter2
Fabric Upgrade

A New Fabric is needed

As you read the first chapter, you may have thought that I have myself become cynical or disillusioned. I am not ! Instead, I am hopeful we can turn it upside down (literally, as we will see in the rest of this book) !

I believe wholeheartedly that we can address many of those issues by reinventing how we think about our corporate fabrics. In fact, I would like to propose an entirely new fabric.

The models we have used are becoming obsolete to a large extent. And while one may argue that they have allowed to create unprecedented prosperity and wealth in the world over the last 30 years, the truth is that it did so at our expense, bringing so much suffering and disengagement in the workplace.

A new fabric is also needed for companies to become more agile in today's world and respond to opportunities and competitive threats far quicker. The speed required in today's marketplace is rapidly accelerating as the world becomes more global and digitized every day.

In addition, as companies welcome a younger workforce with millennials expecting to fully express themselves at work, we need to propose an entirely new corporate fabric.

One in which personal and organizational transformation are intertwined and benefit each other, leading to stronger and more sustainable performance while keeping our people engaged.

The proposed fabric

The new corporate fabric that I am suggesting is based on a new paradigm.

For companies to achieve greater level of engagement, hence performance and innovation, their leaders need to upgrade both themselves and their organizational fabric (culture, decision making, processes, power distribution, mindset, behaviors and accountability level, engagement…)

Both "upgrades" go hand in hand, benefiting each other's transformation processes, leading to more soulful and purpose-driven human beings, employees, managers and organizations . And, as a result, to higher levels of performance.

This is completely different from what is done today which consists for the most part in superimposing change, innovation and engagement programs on top of obsolete fabric. We have it all wrong.

We first need to upgrade our fabric, through radical individual and organizational transformations before we can begin to embark on those programs. People and organizations alike need to be resilient and adaptive enough to be able to evolve with speed, agility and purpose. This is not a small feat !

But the rewards can be immense. What if we could transform our workplaces to become more joyful, soulful and purposeful. Reading that last sentence may very well meet resistance and disbelief because all we have known since we started our career are possibly the exact opposite.

The good news ? There is a path towards this vision which suggests that we need to upgrade ourselves and our organizations. Simultaneously, both processes benefiting each other.

I have visually represented that path below through an ascending lemniscate.

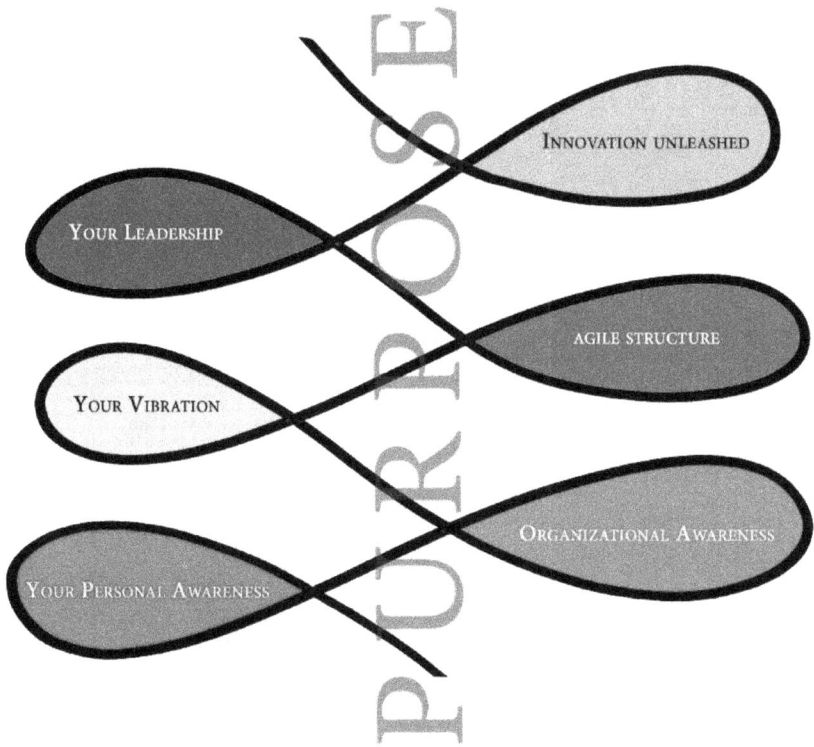

Following that path is not something esoteric or conceptual. It is a very pragmatic set of transformational steps which ultimately leads to soulful workplaces as expression of our talents and purpose.

It takes courage as with any profound transformational journey. But that journey can also be joyful as it frees us and allows us to reveal our potential. Same will apply to organizations.

And the resulting fabric is something which I think can radically transform how we look at our work, our jobs, our companies, our colleagues and managers.

Let's now then joyfully embark on that path, starting, like with any transformation, with awareness. Personal and organizational.

Towards the new fabric

The new corporate fabric has to be redesigned, and this happens through a very dynamic transformational process.

First, it starts with awareness.

Personal awareness : people need to develop a better sense of who they are, how they operate, act and react, how they even have been unconsciously programmed, and how they can change their own "code", if it limits them in what they do and how they do it. We will later look at ways we can become more mindful and aware.

Then, **organizational awareness:** similarly, stakeholders need to understand how their organization operates. We tend to take our environment, processes and culture for granted, and very rarely question them. But before we embark on any organizational transformation, we need to start to be aware of how decisions are being made, how alignment takes place (or not), how the authority is delegated (or not), how tasks are assigned and measured, ... Just to name a few. Interestingly, personal awareness and organizational awareness are intertwined in that they both influence and benefit each other mutually. People with a greater sense of personal awareness will start to better sense whether their existing structure and processes constraint and disempower them. Likewise, a more empowering organization will not get in the way of limiting people's sense of accountability, creativity and urge to do the right thing.

The next stage on our path to more liberating organizations and liberated employees is for both to step up to their full potential. For all of us to step up as the individual leaders and creators we all are and can be, and for our organizations to be resilient, agile and empowering, a radical transformational upgrade needs to happen. **Inwards first, and then outwards**. As an ascending movement, represented in the lemniscate shown earlier.

At a personal level, it starts with our **personal vibration** (which I will expand on a lot more in its dedicated chapter). This is where we gain clarity about our needs, about our unique brilliance, about what we fully want. Ultimately, clarity about how our personal dominant vibration, which allows us to act as a magnet and attract success and passion in our professional lives. And better results !

Likewise, at an organizational level, and once the organization is permeated with vibrant stakeholders, a similar evolution needs to happen inwards, whereby a new social operating system needs to be implemented. We will specifically look at Holacracy as a way to radically evolve our fabric's operating system. This is where the organization gains **agility**. Vibrant employees and creators thrive in a structure which in turn can now fully morph into its original design: adaptive and agile.

As we continue upward, once the fabric's soil and foundations are both resilient and agile, both at a personal and

organizational level, the fabric can now fully expand outward. And serve its purpose.

This is where people start to act as **leaders**, with authenticity, empathy and trust, unafraid of healthy conflicts so that things are done efficiently. Yes, we can all act as leaders, once we have developed a stronger level of personal awareness, and a stronger vibration. And in organizations which are now liberating.

This is finally when optimal performance and constant innovation can take place. I have retained the word **innovation** at this stage because in today's world, this has increasingly become the key to sustainable success.

Ultimately, this ascending virtuous movement will lead to a more soulful and purposeful fabric where both team members and the organization, all seen as living entities, can serve their **purpose**.

Chapter 3
Personal awareness

Our Programming

Awareness is the key we all need to unlock the path to our transformation. Until we are aware of something, we cannot really change or transform it. That seems obvious, but in my experience as a coach and people manager, and as someone we has been spending many years trying to identify and address his own patterns, beliefs and limitations, I can say that this is far from easy. True awareness is more challenging than it sounds. Superficially, we can occasionally say that we are "impatient", sometimes "angry" or "not empathic enough" and "that we could listen more". We all have our challenges, haven't we ?

What I am talking about is different though. I am talking about a deeper level of awareness, one that will invite you to go deeper and deeper, all the way to the root cause of the issues that limit you.

Self awareness is often defined as knowing one's internal states, preferences, resources and intuitions. That requires an unshakable resolve in order not to stay at the surface of things. It requires a detective mind to relentlessly dig up what gets in your way, what makes you react the way you always react . The goal is then to be able to become more conscious and make more conscious choices. So that we go from compulsion and reaction to choice.

Let's say a manager finds it difficult to be fully present and attentive when he meets with his team members. He might be "aware " of it, he could even try hard to listen as intensely as possible in his next one-to-one, but I can bet this will not be enough and not sustainable . The fact that he is "trying" is certainly an encouraging start, but self-awareness goes deeper. He would need to question why that is ? Is there a need to control things ? A need to always be on the lookout for issues, threats, risks ? Difficulty to fully allow things to be and flow ? To be fully present to the other person's needs and feelings ? To be vulnerable ?

You see, like peeling an onion, layer after layer, developing that level awareness can be a journey in itself.

We need to look at our programming from a distance, and discern how our fears and needs often run our life. We can learn to minimize our need to control, to look good, to fit in, to be strong, to be impeccable, on top of things …

What I found though is that ultimately what gets in our way usually find its root in fear-based programming. Our "personal program", which for the most part has been seeded and built until the age of 7, encodes the way we see the world and how we react emotionally to the situations that are thrown at us.

It is therefore crucial to develop the necessary discernment to track down our fear-based beliefs and reactions. Given work situations can sometimes be highly emotionally charged, and offer countless opportunities to be triggered to react unconsciously, being aware of our fear-based patterns and conditioning become critical.

Fear-based behaviors

Here are a few examples of fear-based behaviors we might encounter at work. This is by no means exhaustive!

Fear-Based
Be visible at all cost
Always tell people what to do and how to do it
Protect you by securing everyone's buy-in
Go through extensive and lengthy review processes
Command & Control
Keep information to your chest
Decision pushed to the top
Politics
Be reaction-driven

All of them will find their origin in fear and our egos.

Once again, let me use an excerpt from Frederic Laloux in his book "Reinventing Organizations"

> *"Taming the ego could have deep repercussions on how we structure and run organizations. Many of the corporate ills today can be traced to behaviors driven by fearful egos: politics, bureaucratic rules and processes, endless meetings, analysis paralysis, information hoarding and secrecy, wishful thinking, ignoring problems away, lack of authenticity, silos and infighting, decision-making concentrated at the top of organizations, and so forth."*

Does it sound like something we all have experienced at work?

A lot of our fear-based actions and reactions have to do with our worldview. Can we consider different type of behaviors although we have been entrenched in ours for so many years? Probably since we have started to work, or even since our parents did. Many companies today are mostly ego-driven. The shift to a different kind of fabric can only happen when we learn to dis-identify from our own ego and our fear.

Here, I would like to briefly discuss what « ego » means as there might be some confusion about what I mean by it. I have met with several leaders over the years who believe that « having a strong ego » is indeed a good thing. As a matter of fact, they felt that this was one of the key qualities managers should be able to display in order   to   lead.

The way I look at the ego is very simply everything which leads to separation. Separation from others, from self even. And there are so many ways in which we act that bring separation: Judgment, blame, resentment, talking about others, putting ourselves or others on a pedestal, … Many spiritual teachings describe the path to liberation from the ego as a path towards unity. Therefore, "having a strong ego" can be misleading. Assertiveness expressed consciously can indeed be a great "tool" as long as it is not meant to bring more separation !

Giving power to the ego can indeed be very damaging as it « consumes » so much of our energy in activities that are counter-productive. Our egos often do a very good job at separating us from what is. At work, this can take many different forms: forcing our point of view, thinking as « we-they » or « I-He/She » , as « I win-He loses » or vice versa.

So, what does it look like to be driven, not by fear, but by a higher purpose, a sense of wholeness, our soul ? A sense of possibilities and abundance. If something positive happens to a colleague, it does not deprive you of anything. The universe is abundant and good things do not happen at the detriment of others. You trust that you can react more consciously and that this will lead to a better life for you and those around you.

If all you have known in your professional life are workplaces where politics and conflicts were the rule, it may be nearly impossible to consider that something else can exist. And that has to do with our worldview. Do we see the world as a place of dangers where we are better off protecting ourselves from external (perceived) risks (.i.e separation) or a place where we can take bold steps towards authenticity, vulnerability, trust and wholeness ?

The good news ? There are ways, even tools to help us develop a greater level of discernment about ourselves, a greater level of self-awareness. This is a practice called mindfulness.

Mindfulness will indeed give you that space from which you can indeed look from a distance, and witness your patterns and behaviors.

The Good news

Would you agree that our workplace can really be a place of intense emotions ?
Sure, it is a place of opportunities for personal achievements, success, camaraderie and even fun. But like in other areas of our lives, it can also be the crucible of intense emotions. For instance,

- Have you ever felt resentful of a colleague or your boss ?
- Obsessed by what someone else told you ? Or by the thought he is possibly even instigating something against you?
- Or fear of being fired or not being promoted ?
- Or sadness and anger for not being recognized , valued and appreciated?

Going through emotions is just part of our lives, isn't it ? The issue at work though is that we tend to react to them in ways that can be harmful. To us and to others too.
And because we are neurologically wired a certain way, we will tend to respond to emotional situations almost always the same way, driven by our old patterns, beliefs and habits.
For instance, we will react by blaming others. Or blaming ourselves.
Other people will decide instead to fight back creating more confusion.
They might start to behave in some obsessive ways. Or just go silent and suck it all up. Or go in panic mode.

The truth is that in most cases the response to the situation will rarely result into something productive or appropriate. And will almost never lead to the resolution of what may have caused conflicts, frustration or anger in the first place.

In today's work environment, where things are changing so rapidly and frequently (technologies, organizations, competition …), we will all need to develop a new set of skills. Sure, we will always need to develop "business skills" . But emotional intelligence and awareness are essential assets we will increasingly need to navigate our corporate world. In my experience as a manager, some of the most important skills that make us more successful at work are our ability to connect to our inner life, our emotional and mental awareness. Connection to both our emotions and to our mind is required.

In a famous poem, 13th century Sufi poet Rumi beautifully depicts how best welcoming difficult emotions in life, rather than avoiding them. I could not think of a better way to illustrate what we will discuss next.

This being human is a guest-house.
Every morning a new arrival.
A joy, a depression, meanness,
some momentary awareness comes
as an unexpected visitor.
Welcome and entertain them all!
Even if they're a crowd of sorrows,
Who violently sweep your house
empty of its furniture.
still, treat each guest honorably.
He may be clearing you
out for some new delight.
The dark thought, the shame, the malice,

meet them at the door laughing,
and invite them in.
Be grateful for whoever comes,
because each has been sent
as a guide from beyond.
–Rumi, "The Guest House"

Daniel Goldman defined Emotional Intelligence as 5 interrelated domains :

1. Emotional self-awareness — knowing what one is feeling at any given time and understanding the impact those moods have on others
2. Self-regulation — controlling or redirecting one's emotions; anticipating consequences before acting on impulse
3. Motivation — utilizing emotional factors to achieve goals, enjoy the learning process and persevere in the face of obstacles
4. Empathy — sensing the emotions of others
5. Social skills — managing relationships, inspiring others and inducing desired responses from them

In other words:

1. Knowing your emotions.
2. Managing your own emotions.
3. Motivating yourself.
4. Recognizing and understanding other people's emotions.
5. Managing relationships.

The « good » news is that, although we might at times feel we are victim of our emotions, emotional skills are trainable. Those skills can then be helpful in our response to triggers (a colleague strongly disagrees with you), during difficult conversations (with your customers, or with your team members) and in developing our ability to deal with stressful situations (in period of changes for instance).

This is where mindfulness can help us developing those skills. There are many resources on mindfulness available online as it is gaining tremendous traction in the corporate world now (a very good example would be the success of the "Search Inside Yourself" program at Google or the increasingly popular "Wisdom 2.0" conference). At a very high level, mindfulness is the practice of a certain form of meditation used (among other things) to bring emotional balance as well as peace to our mind.

Jon Kabat-Zinn defines mindfulness as "paying attention in a particular way; On purpose, in the present moment, and non-judgmentally."
Kabat-Zinn, if you have not heard of him, is a teacher of mindfulness meditation and the founder of the Mindfulness-Based Stress Reduction program at the University of Massachusetts Medical Center.
Now, let me be clear. The objective here is not to suppress emotions! There is no way to stop an emotion from arising, that is part of our lives and kind of what makes us human. Mindfulness will help us to get closer to our emotions while clearly understanding that we are not defined by them (in other words, moving for instance from « I am angry » to « I experience anger in me»).

By developing an ability to pay attention to our inner life we become more emotionally stable and grounded.

Mindfulness not only helps with emotional intelligence, but is a key tool to access our agitated mind. It is said we have about 60000 thoughts/day, of which only 0.5% are conscious thoughts! Our mind thinks us, not the other way around! Mindfulness, as a way to pay attention more consciously, develops a different way of being by helping us to regain mastery of our thoughts. And start to think consciously!

At work, in difficult situations, to what extent are we responding by making conscious choices instead of merely reproducing the same old responses, colored by the same old emotional imprints!?

In work situations, we will instead develop more awareness about how we make decisions, and move from compulsion to choice. Choice of our emotional response, for instance. We develop an ability to have a different perspective on things, see the bigger picture as we manage over time to be less entrenched in our emotions by reframing difficult situations. And ultimately start to look at other people's point of view, which leads to empathy (as we shall discuss later).

I would now like to share concrete tools and techniques that are really helpful to develop increased awareness to our inner life and a stronger sense of presence. And as a result, more appropriate responses and behaviors to emotionally challenging situations at work.

Practical tool-1

Now, although its benefits are clear and tangible (as neuroscience has shown through numerous studies conducted over the past 15 years), the practice of mindfulness and meditation requires stamina and perseverance.

Our modern hectic lives don't always give us the chance to sit in meditation at 4 a.m for hours like a Tibetan monk in the Himalayas, do they?

So what do we do? Where do we start?

The very good news is that it simply starts with you, now.

Yes, you can find online many guided mindfulness meditations. But even guided meditations can be difficult to begin with. Here is a very simple way to get you started:

Sit comfortably, and try to be alert and relax at the same time.

– Closing your eyes, start to take 3 long breaths.

– Then, start to pay attention to your breath, following the inhale and the exhale.

– If that helps to ground your focus, you can also pay attention to the sensation at the tip of your nose as the air goes in and out through your nose and your lungs.

– If the mind gets agitated (and it will !), when you realize you started to get lost in your thoughts, gently come back to the breath. Without any judgment or attachment.

– Start to also pay attention to the bodily sensations, by mentally scanning different parts of your body. Do you notice contractions?

That's it. 5 mins, every day.

Although it has been shown that a daily practice of at least 20 mins brings more benefits, simply doing the above for only 5 mins a day will make a big difference.

How were you when you started 5 mins ago? How are you now? Do you notice a difference in the quality of your thoughts? Your emotions?

Now, you might ask yourself : "that is great, but how do I do that at work? I go from one meeting to another, I do not have any time for that !"

Well, first, I am sure you can find 5 mins in your day, right? Why not setting your clock or a reminder on your computer ? At a time when you know you can have 5 mins. It could be when you arrive in the office ? Or before you actually go to work? Or just before lunch time ? As long as you do not close your eyes while in your car, you should be fine!

One last comment.

Say you manage to establish a routine. And are experiencing difficulties in your life (at work or elsewhere). You might drop your practice, because those difficulties can be challenging or even overwhelming. And as result, you might decide to stop your practice for one day, one week, or even months. That is ok ! The same way you go back to your breath when you get distracted, simply notice without any judgment or self-criticism that indeed you have stopped your practice. And gently reestablish it.

Over time, you will be able to notice differences in how you go through your day at work (and elsewhere) when you have been able to maintain a regular practice and when you have not. And your colleagues or team members might notice it too.

Practical tool-2

Let's now look at another very concrete way of being more mindful and bringing peace in difficult work situations.

RAIN is an acronym for the four key principles of mindful transformation of difficulties. RAIN stands for Recognition, Acceptance, Investigation, and Non-identification and stems from Eastern spiritual practices. The short explanation below of the RAIN process is mostly taken from book excerpts from Jack Kornfield and Tara Brach.

RAIN directs our attention in a clear, systematic way that cuts through confusion and stress. The 4 steps give us somewhere to turn in any painful moment. Like the clear sky and clean air after a cooling rain, this mindfulness practice brings a new openness and calm to our daily lives.

Recognition is the first step of mindfulness. When we feel stuck, we must begin with a willingness to see what is so. It is as if someone asks us gently, "What is happening now?" Do we reply brusquely, "Nothing"? Or do we pause and acknowledge the reality of our experience, here and now? With recognition we step out of denial. Denial undermines our freedom.

The next step of RAIN is **acceptance**. Acceptance allows us to relax and open to the facts before us. It is necessary because with recognition there can come a subtle aversion, a resistance, a wish it weren't so. Acceptance does not mean that we cannot work to improve things. But just now, this is what is so. Problems that seemed intractable often become now workable.

In recognition and acceptance we recognize our dilemma and accept the truth of the whole situation. But you may need to further awaken and strengthen mindful awareness with the I of RAIN.

Starting with **investigation** in the body, we mindfully locate where our difficulties are held. In the second foundation of mindfulness, we can investigate what feelings are part of this difficulty. Is the primary feeling tone pleasant, unpleasant, or neutral? Are we meeting this feeling with mindfulness? Next comes the mind. What thoughts and images are associated with this difficulty? What stories, judgments, and beliefs are we holding? When we look more closely, we can discover that many of them are one-sided, fixed points of view or outmoded, habitual perspectives. When we see that they are only stories, they loosen their hold on us. We cling less to them.

And finally, N. **Non-identification** means that your sense of who you are is not fused with or defined by any limited set of emotions, sensations or stories. In non-identification we stop taking the experience as "mine" or part of "me." We see how identification creates dependence, anxiety, and inauthenticity. This is the culmination of releasing difficulty through RAIN.

Let' s now look at an example taken from a work situation to make it more concrete.
Say, Paul, has been hoping to get a new job which had just been opened within his company. But unfortunately, he is not getting it as it is given instead to someone more senior, although less experienced in that particular field. Paul goes through an intense emotional storm (denial, anger, hatred, sadness, guilt, blame…). He is also entrenched in thoughts such as quitting, going to the hiring manager to take out his anger, looking at ways the hired person could fail, deciding on how he would ignore him the next time he meets with him, etc …I let you use your creativity here to complete the list!
In other words, Paul's reptilian brain is fully at work!

Going through the RAIN process would allow him instead to find different response strategies to the painful and challenging situation.

40

R: Paul could start by fully acknowledging the reality of the situation. Despite his efforts, he is not getting the job and the potential salary increase he was counting on. That is the reality, now.

A: Accept the situation. It could be helpful to take a few deep breathes, in a silent environment, and let the reality sink. That step certainly could be difficult, but moving to acceptance is a key step. Which Paul might need to go through a few times.

I: This is the heart of the mindfulness practice. Simply observing the emotions and thoughts as well as bodily sensations. And be curious about what is at play ? Has he reacted similarly in the past ? Any alternative coping strategy emerging ?

N: Paul sees how the internal drama is happening automatically, almost without him being involved. As a result of old imprints. And can start to dissociate from it.

The workplace can be very challenging at times. RAIN can be of great help in those situations, and I know colleagues who benefited tremendously from this practice.

Chapter 4
Organizational Awareness

Similarly, we need to question our organizations and develop a sense of how things work and get done. In my experience, this is very rarely questioned or even discussed. While leaders will occasionally evolve the org charts and (more rarely) the organization's governance, we usually do not challenge how things are done. We may elude the question altogether by saying "oh, this is simply part of our culture!", but one needs to develop a much stronger sense of organizational awareness. The same way we become more aware at a personal level as discussed in the previous chapter, we also need to question our organizational structure and processes.

- What is our structure ? Formal and informal ? Does the structure allow us to get things done more efficiently ? How is control and alignment done ?
- How are decisions made ? How fast ?
- What is the level of accountability in the company ? How transparent are roles, initiatives and projects ?

Question your structure

How often have you heard that the complexity in your company structures or organizations is getting in the way ? That they are just too complex ? Prevent people from getting things done ?
First, and from my experience, we very often blame our structures without even understanding or questioning them in the first place. And second, it is often a question of having the right structure for what the organizations, teams or business units need to achieve.
The organizational specialist, Elliott Jaques, identifies three distinct types of structure: the formal structure, the extant structure and the requisite structure.

The **"formal" structure:** this is where we find the org chart and the job descriptions. Do you even remember what is in your job description, if you are lucky enough to have one. No one is really aware of his own, nor is using other people's job description to see whether he would be the most appropriate person to perform a specific tasks or contribute to a project? There is an abyss between what we formally have in our job description and how things get done, and by whom.

When the organization's formal structure offers little guidance on what is actually needed day to day, we humans work around the formal structure to get the job done. This gives rise to another kind of structure, which Jaques calls the **"extant structure."** This is the structure that is actually operating—the often implicit reality of who's making what decisions, who owns which projects, and so on. As we work together in this way, cultural norms develop, and we start aligning with those, creating an implicit structure that becomes the often unconscious "way things are done."

by Mark Walsh from Integration Training

I have posted this chart by Mark Walsh which you will find online. One because I found it absolutely hilarious, and two, because it shows what an extant structure could be in reality ! Needless to

45

say, it might actually be quite far from your formal structure or your requisite structure which I will discuss next.

Elliott Jaques then defines a third structure: the **"requisite structure"** which is the structure that would be most natural and best suited to the work and purpose of the organization.

Organizational awareness starts by questioning the three types of structure briefly discussed here. How are each type at work in your company ? How formal or informal ? Are they getting in the way?

That would be a good starting point as those structures have deep repercussions on what I would like to discus next, which is the decision making processes and the levels of accountability and empowerment found in organizations.

Decision making

"We need to find a consensus with the leadership team before we move on".

"Have you reached consensus with all stakeholders on this initiative ?"

Does it sound familiar?

I will not go through here why seeking consensus when making decision is not very effective nor does create alignment and buy-in. Trying to reach consensus is, in most cases, sub-optimal and rarely secures actual commitment.

As part of the organizational awareness stage we are discussing here, it is always a good practice to reflect on your decision making process. It does makes sense, of course, to solicit different opinions and perspectives before moving full speed ahead. But trying to reach a consensus, and include everyone's suggestions and inputs can very quickly lead to paralysis. And often, by the time you reach unanimity, one of two things can happen : the proposal or project has lost its relevance or impact, or because so much time was needed to make the decision, it could very well be too late.

I understand why we do that at work: we have the need to secure buy-in, in other words, the need to protect ourselves in case something goes wrong. But in my experience, reaching consensus at all cost is … very expensive !

There are emerging governance methods in the market place today (holacracy, which we will discuss soon, being one of them), which aim at tackling that kind of paralysis.

Dynamic governance is a decision-making and governance method that allows an organization to manage itself as an organic whole. To make this possible, dynamic governance enables every sub-part of the organization to have an authoritative voice in the management of the organization.

And it will rely on consent (as opposed to consensus). Consent can be defined as the principle which governs decision-making. Consent means no argued and paramount objection. In other words, a policy decision can only be made if nobody has a reasoned and paramount objection to it.

In short, consent means decisions are being collectively made when there is "zero-objection" left. And objections need to be argued.

Consensus does not really work, as it is almost impossible to get everyone to say "yes" to a proposal which , by the way, also needs to fulfill their individual needs. Instead, consent is about having the persons involved in the decision process able to live with the proposal within their own limits of tolerance. If the proposal does not fulfill their needs (that is, it is outside the limits of what they can tolerate, accept, or adhere to), they will have the chance to propose an argued objection, which will then be taken into consideration by the circle to improve the proposal.

Consent is based on the quality of the arguments rather than on proving who is right or wrong. It develops a specific energy whereby team members carefully listen to the objections, and seek to explore how to integrate them to come to a better joint proposition. No winner, no loser, the team wins instead!

True leaders understand that their authority and influence do not come from only making top-down decisions, but those who will be more inclusive. Very often, their proposals may actually turn to be the "best" ones, given their insight and perspective due to their experience and position in the company. But not always...
The benefits of inclusion by seeking consent rather than consensus are a stronger buy-in, better decisions being made, faster execution, better productivity and a more engaged workforce.

We work in increasingly collaborative environments, providing fantastic opportunities to tap into our teams' collective intelligence, and yet, the way we take decisions and apply them is still very much centralized and top-down.
Models exist to develop more inclusive decision-making processes and design different organizations to ensure better decisions, stronger buy-in, sharper execution and sense of belonging. We will discuss them later in the book.

In my experience, the way decisions are made is a good indicator and a good place to start.

Same goes for what I would like to discuss now, that is, the level of accountability and empowerment.

Accountability and Sensing Tension

How much do you think people in your organization feel accountable for what they are supposed to do ?

In addition, in case they see a "tension", that is, a gap between what is and what should be, how likely are they going to do something about it ? Or even just raise it ?

I have picked those two because I have found them both to be very strong indicators of your existing fabric's "health". They both give a sense of how people feel empowered and willing to take things into their own hands.

Accountability

The challenge with accountability is that our workplaces are filled with ... implicit expectations.

No job description or document will tell stakeholders what to expect from any one of us. We constantly rely on implicit expectations all the time, and same goes for any of our colleagues about us. We must expect things of each other to work together effectively.

When someone comply to what we expect from her, all is good. But when he does not, that creates invariably frustration and resentment as this can have important consequences for the project or task we are accountable for. One side effect is the increased time we will spend in politics. You end up spending a lot of energy and time ensuring the implicit expectations you have come as close as possible of being explicit! You start to spend a lot of time influencing others, securing buy-in, etc, etc .. While this is part of any organization, sure, you may want to challenge how much time is spent in those kind of internal politics and alignment.

If you have a strong culture of accountability , that is, one in which people act on implicit expectations by proactively clarifying them with their stakeholders, things ultimately get done.
But if not, you may want to investigate and question the accountability level of your organization. Because otherwise, this creates a disempowered culture. People start to understand that very little can be done without huge amount of energy spent in just reaching some consensus. And then, will either just rely on their managers or leaders to do it, or just let things fall through the cracks.

To me, nothing is worse that teams or organizations that do not care enough not to drop things they know should be taken care of. And you need to become aware whether this happens within your organization, or is about to happen.

Tension

Which leads to me to this idea of tension, borrowed from Holacracy.
In Holacracy, tension describes a person's felt sense that there is a gap between the current reality and a potential future.
For instance, you have just met with 5 new customers this week, and 4 are giving you the same mixed feedback about your product

quality. Or are suggesting the same improvements about your services.

Clearly, as the salesperson, you feel that there is a tension that should be addressed or raised internally.

And in our organizational life, we are likely to face many tensions on a daily basis. It could be about specific actions, or about specific processes. Or even a tension you sense has something to do with your company strategy, possibly after you have heard information about an imminent move from one of your competitors.

As you seek to develop more organizational awareness, it is critical you know what happens when members of your organization sense tensions. What do they do about them ?

In my book "Ecological Leadership", I used the analogy with what happens in Mother Nature, in living systems and ecosystems. Those systems are remarkable at adapting to tensions through reacting, responding, morphing or evolving. In a well oiled fabric, tensions are processed for the good of the company and should be warning signs to help it to evolve. Fro instance, reacting to competitive threats or detecting new market opportunities.

All stakeholders need to be able to rely on a very responsive and accountable fabric, one that senses and responds to tensions.Why ? At a leader's level, it is likely that he is on top of only the top 3-5 high priorities he really needs to drive for the company. But in today's modern marketplace, you have to be able to sense and respond to a lot more tensions that those falling into the leader's top 5. It is a question of survival and adaptation.

The challenge is that we usually do not have a place to go to process those tensions. There is no formal process to log and discuss tensions, and that can very quickly turn into many lost opportunities.

The risk then become that over time people increasingly find it difficult to cope with unresolved tensions, and then, end up not caring anymore about doing something !

We will later see how Holacracy offers a forum for those tensions to be processed, but you need to know where your organization stands when it comes to sensing and responding.

Chapter 5
Your vibration

Once both personal and organizational awareness have been developed, it is time to "move up the stack" (as depicted with the lemniscate)   and become a stronger and more active agent of transformation. For yourself first, and then for your organization. And we will first look at it inward. What do I mean by that?

From a personal standpoint, and for your corporate fabric to be as soulful and performant as possible, I believe that members of that fabric (the team members, the managers and the leaders) need to all become strong vibrational individuals. Aware of their dominant vibrations, through a more acute sense of their feelings, needs and strengths, a clear understanding of what they want to achieve for themselves and for their teams.

People with substance, presence. This is a prerequisite to what we will discuss at a later stage, true personal leadership. The reason I categorize it as "inward" versus "outward" (personal leadership) is that this has to do a lot more with introspection as well as with developing and maintaining one's personal vibration. Whereas leadership will be applied outward, towards others, teams and customers…

But let's not jump too fast here, and let's first examine the path to our dominant vibration so that we can all be fully empowered and strong agents of our companies' fabric.

In my experience, that path goes through three important milestones:

1. Being clear about your own feelings and needs, and be able to communicate them clearly. Without anger or without being in conflicting mode, while being empathic with other's feelings and needs.
2. Understanding what your strengths are and cultivate them to elevate you to your unique brilliance
3. Vibrating powerfully by knowing, expressing (and aiming at) what you want as opposed to what you do not want.

We will first examine the importance of being clear about our feelings and needs, as well as being able to fully communicate them.

The Importance of your needs

Being clear on our needs, communicating them, understanding each other's needs and act consciously and emphatically upon them is that magic key that I found can unlock the path to fulfilling relationships.

At work, this is really important. Workplaces can very quickly become places of resentment, anger and frustration when we let inauthentic relationships to develop. Our ego takes over, and very quickly, we lose sight of the fact that we all are here with the same needs. Need for belonging, for creating or for achieving great things, just to name a few.

In addition, in my experience as coach and manager, stress and burnout happen primarily when our needs are not met. And when we do not or can not express our brilliance. The reality though is that we are not used to pay enough attention to them, and even will tend to meet other people's needs. I really believe that we need to develop that specific muscle, being aware of our feelings and needs first, communicating them and being able to listen to each other's needs and feelings. So that we can become part of a stronger fabric of empowered individuals, not afraid of vulnerability, disagreement or conflicts.

What I found is that as you start to take care of your own needs, you become more whole. Which will in turn make you more successful as your relationships become less polluted by unnecessary defensive mechanisms or politics.

That is why I have decided to reproduce part of a chapter on "Nonviolent Communication" I wrote in my previous book,

"Ecological Leadership". Based on the many feedback I have received, I realized that building that muscle had indeed been a key for many. And in the workplace, even more so, as we are constantly being asked (whether this is happening consciously or unconsciously) to fit in and comply.

Nonviolent Management

Few years back, I discovered the Nonviolent Communication (NVC) practice through a couple of books and started to use it empirically. I then decided to attend several weekend trainings on NVC.

Day after day, I could witness how powerful and enriching this process is, both in my relationships and communication at work as well as in my personal life. While the process is simple to grasp, it takes effort before you can start to forget it, like with any new muscles you are trying to develop. As you keep practicing, you will witness the unfolding of profound transformation.

At work, NVC can be used practically in all interactions and meetings. I will provide many examples throughout this chapter that are specific to workplaces so that you can also learn how to use it.

As managers, leaders or individual contributors, benefits are huge. By taking care of the ecology within you and others, and meeting your needs and others' needs, you nurture and build relationships that have a different quality. Less judgment, evaluation and blame.

And as a result, you reach new levels of engagement and productivity, for yourself in your job, and for your teams, if you are a people manager.

From the NVC website[4] :

"Nonviolent Communication is based on historical principles of nonviolence– the natural state of compassion when no violence is present in the heart. NVC reminds us what we already instinctively know about how good it feels to authentically connect to another human being.

With NVC we learn to hear our own deeper needs and those of others. Through its emphasis on deep listening—to ourselves as well as others—NVC helps us discover the depth of our own compassion. This language reveals the awareness that all human beings are only trying to honor universal values and needs, every minute, every day.

NVC can be seen as both a spiritual practice that helps us see our common humanity, using our power in a way that honors everyone's needs, and a concrete set of skills which help us create life-serving families and communities. The form is simple, yet powerfully transformative.

Through the practice of NVC, we can learn to clarify what we are observing, what emotions we are feeling, what values we want to live by, and what we want to ask of others and ourselves. We will no longer need to use the language of blame, judgment or domination. We can experience the deep pleasure of contributing to each other's well being.

NVC creates a path for healing and reconciliation in its many applications, ranging from intimate relationships, work settings, health care, social services, police, prison staff and inmates, to governments, schools and social change organizations."

Let's explore deeper the skills needed to create "life-serving" teams and organizations.

---

[4] http://www.cnvc.org/

Nonviolent Communication 101

Before we look at how NVC can be applied at work, I need to go through some of the key concepts. The best introduction on the topic remains the book "Nonviolent Communication: A Language of Life" from Marshall Rosenberg, founder of NVC.

I will simply highlight the basic principles so that you can better understand some of the areas and examples throughout the rest of the chapter, and why those skills are important in the workplace.

NVC Concept and Examples

The model involves the following four steps:

NVC Steps	
1. Objective Observation (observation without judgment) **- Concrete actions I observe, without analysis**	"When I (see, hear, remember, imagine, etc.)…"
2. Honest Feelings[13] (from inside oneself) **- How I feel in relation to these actions**	"I feel…"
3. Universal Needs[14] **- The life energy in the form of needs, desires, wishes, or values that creates my feelings.**	"Because I am (needing)…"
4. Specific, Present, Doable Requests **- Clearly requesting what would enrich my life and the life of others without demanding. The concrete actions I would like to be taken.**	"Would you be willing to…?"

As you can see, it is not about judging, blaming, evaluating others, but about taking responsibility for your own feelings, needs and requests, based on clear observations:

"When I see…, I feel… because I am needing/valuing… Would you be willing to...?"

And not: "When you do …, you are really .. because you always …"

Lets' have a look at an example; you will see immediately the difference!

A: "You never listen to me when I'm talking to you. You're ignoring me constantly. You just don't care!"

B: "Yeah right! I listen to you all the time!"

A: "You can't listen to me and read the paper at the same time! You're so unreal!"

B: "I'm unreal?! You don't even…. "

(Discussion goes nowhere and ends in frustration)

Now, let's see, and almost feel, the difference in the following conversation:

A: "When I see you read the newspaper while I'm talking, I feel frustrated because I'm needing to be heard. Would you be willing to close the newspaper for 5 minutes and hear my idea?"
B: "When you ask me to close the paper when I'm reading an article that is very important to me I feel anxious because of my need to understand what's going on in the world. I also feel concerned because of my need for your well-being. Would you be willing to wait 5 minutes while I finish this article so I can give you my full attention?"
A: "Yes"

Based on the above, there are then essentially 2 ways of moving toward connection:

2 ways of moving toward connection
1. Honestly express your own feelings & needs Ongoing awareness of feelings & connected needs in present moment Willingness & courage to express those feelings & needs (vulnerability)
2. Empathically listen to other's feelings & needs Qualities of empathic listening: presence, focus, space, caring, verbal reflection of feelings & needs NOT advising, fixing, consoling, story-telling, sympathizing, analyzing, explaining, … No matter what is said, hear only feelings, needs, observations & requests

And that is really the core of NVC. Our choice, moment by moment, to have fulfilling connections with others, choosing alternatively one of those two ways above.

How We Choose to Hear Difficult Messages

Expanding on the key concepts above, NVC describes 4 ways we choose to hear difficult messages.

Attack Myself	Attack her
I judge and blame myself	*I judge and blame the other person*
I take it personally	*I turn what I hear against the other person*
I am wrong	*I accuse the other person, she is wrong*
SHAME-GUILT-DEPRESSION	ANGER
What I tell myself (Impressions, judgments)	What I think of the other person (impressions judgments)
Listen to myself	**Listen to her**
Self-Empathy	*Empathy*
LISTEN TO MYSELF	LISTEN TO THE OTHER PERSON
"When I see…,	
I feel…	"When you say…,
because I am needing/valuing…	Do you feel…
Would you be willing to…?"	because you are needing/valuing…
	Would you be willing to tell me what is going on…?"

Let's have a look at the example below. I am sure you can find plenty of similar examples drawn from your experiences at work!

Person A: How dare you walk out of the room when I'm talking! You idiot! You just can't stand to hear the truth.

1. Person B (blaming A): Me the idiot. … How about you! You're the one who started all this in the first place. You are so self-righteous telling me I'm inconsiderate. You've never thought about another human being beside yourself!

2. Person B (blaming himself): Oh, I'm sorry. I didn't mean to be disrespectful. It's just that I don't know what to do. I never know what to do, or what to say. I feel so worthless!

3. Person B (sensing his own feelings/needs): When I hear you say that, I feel hurt because I'm needing respect and to be seen for whom I am. And I really need some space because I'm in a lot of pain right now… Would you be willing to tell me what you heard me just say?

4. Person B (sensing A's feelings/needs): Are you feeling angry and wanting respect and to be heard?

NVC helps us to connect to what is alive within us and within others, moment by moment. It is about reaching win-win situations for both parties with each other's needs fulfilled.

As you can see, the concept is rather simple and as you will see when you start experiencing it, very powerful! NVC can be used effectively in situations of conflicts, tensions, misunderstanding and mediation where creative new solutions are more likely to emerge.

Most of the time, we disagree on "How"(the strategies) we fulfill our needs, NOT the needs themselves, which are identical for most human beings. Once you experience we all have identical needs, communication starts to become a lot more peaceful and compassionate. And solutions can be found more collaboratively, leading to increased productivity and performance.

The art of giving feedback

Giving feedback is one of the most important skills for leaders. Managers very often receive "coaching" or "training" on providing feedback. But most of the "tips" I have seen very often miss the point.

Before we look at how best we can provide constructive and ecological (mindful of the person's feelings and identity) feedback at the same time, let me first emphasize the most important finding I have made through trial and error until I (kind of) got it right: the feedback has to be done on the person's actual behavior, not on the person himself.

Behaviors, not the person

I would like to illustrate that point with a specific type of feedback (Praise), and examine two studies that are very enlightening.

Praise is a powerful and commonly used tool to reinforce positive behavior and motivate employees, but a growing body of research challenges the purely beneficial effects of praising people for success. I have looked at two studies; one with children and another one with students. Results were consistent and... striking.

Conventional wisdom suggests that praising a child as a whole or praising his or her traits is beneficial.

Two studies[5] tested the hypothesis that both criticism and praise that conveyed person or trait judgments could send a message of contingent worth and undermine subsequent coping. In Study 1, 67 children (ages 5-6 years) role-played tasks involving a setback and received 1 of 3 forms of criticism after each task: person, outcome, or process criticism. In Study 2, 64 children role-played successful tasks and received person, outcome, or process praise.

[5] Melissa L. Kamins and Carol S. Dweck, Columbia University

In both studies, self-assessments, affect, and persistence were measured on a subsequent task involving a setback. Results indicated that children displayed significantly more "helpless" responses (including self-blame) on all dependent measures after person criticism or praise than after process criticism or praise. Thus person feedback, even when positive, can create vulnerability and a sense of contingent self-worth.

Therefore, praising the process of a task (e.g., effort, strategy) leads to positive motivational outcomes. Praising the person (e.g., ability, intelligence) can promote negative outcomes after subsequent setbacks, such as uncontrollable attributions, helpless coping and contingent self-worth.

Another study[6] examines how college students react to person and process praise relative to no praise before and after experiencing subsequent failure.
Procedure: Participants worked on 3 puzzles total, receiving high scores on the first two followed by either person praise or process praise (see below). Participants in the control condition received only the numeric feedback.

Person praise: "Great! You're really good at these!" after the first puzzle; "Excellent! You must have a natural talent." after the second.

Process praise: "Great! It seems like you put a lot of effort into these"; "Excellent! You must be using some really effective strategies."
On the third puzzle, participants received a score lower than average and were told "You didn't do as well on this last one." Participants then completed a questionnaire assessing intrinsic motivation, perceived competence, contingent self-worth, and performance attributions.

[6] Kyla Haimovitz & Jennifer Henderlong Corpus; Reed College

After the setback trial, students reported more intrinsic motivation after process praise than after person praise, with the control condition in between. Undergraduates are more motivated by process praise than person praise when later faced with failure.

Consequently, understanding the counterintuitive effects of these commonly used motivators and feedback is really important.
We tend to provide feedback that is solely expressed as person praise, hence speaking to that person's identity. Even giving a positive feedback, such a in "You are really good at presenting to customers" turns out not to effective.
Not everyone has enough self-awareness to make that distinction: "That feedback is not about me as a person, rather about what I did"

Let's then see how we can develop that really important skill of providing more ecological and constructive feedback in the workplace. Mastering that skill will make a huge difference and foster a much stronger level of engagement.

How to give ecological feedback

Nonviolent Communication (NVC) can be a really powerful framework to provide feedback to someone in the context of the workplace.
NVC is about being attentive to both one's feelings and needs while at the same type being fully respectful of ours. Inclusion with empathy!
The frenetic pace at which we sometimes go through our day at work does not usually allow for time and space for constructive and authentic exchanges. We (I certainly do) jump from one meeting to

another, from one priority to another with sometime no presence to others or even ourselves.

At the same time, the nature of our work needs to be increasingly more collaborative and inclusive of others' views and feedback.

As a result, caught by stress, lack of time and conscious presence, we end up saying things like:

"You should pay more attention to details", "you should communicate better" or "you did a great job!". Even saying things like "you did a great job!", which seems like a "great" positive feedback", is a disguised form of judgment and evaluation! Whereby the person is putting herself/himself in a "high" position to deliver a pretty definitive opinion on someone else.

First, compassionate feedback (solicited or unsolicited) must have the quality of the relationship as its most important objective. When it is not the case, the given feedback will most likely speak more of the person providing that feedback rather than serve the person receiving it.

For instance, if a manager who struggles to raise his own team's visibility is saying to someone "you should be more visible", will it really be helpful?

Feedback, as an inclusive process, and as Nonviolent Communication explains, will seek to serve the other person by being very specific on the observed cause and effects, without evaluation or judgment.

Let's now see how we can provide better feedback that is inclusive of both persons' feelings and needs.

1. We do not give feedback on someone, but on **observable behaviors**, which that person has had (very important!).

Therefore, most feedback starting with "YOU should..." is unlikely to be inclusive of the other person's feelings and needs! Instead, we will rather give feedback on the specific cause, that is, the behaviors which have led to a situation. By doing so, we are particularly mindful of distinguishing an observation without judgment from an evaluation. This is a key step in the NVC framework, and equally important when it comes to giving feedback.

2. The consequences and effects.

Here, we will talk about our **needs** that have been fulfilled (or not) by the behaviors and actions of the person. And then, express the **feelings**, which have emerged as a consequence of our needs being fulfilled (or not).

We are here at the heart of NVC. Humans are all moved by needs we all to seek to satisfy. And that our feelings (anger, frustration, fear, despair, sadness...) are like luminous warnings on a car dashboard: they tell us to what extent our needs are fulfilled or not. Hence, when providing feedback, it is always best to indicate to what extent the behavior of the other person has fulfilled my own needs and the feelings they have triggered.

That step is really important: we talk about us, rather than about the other person. Our feedback will consequently be given without a sense of moralization or critics.

3. Optional: at this stage, one could additionally reinforce the consequences that the new behavior will have on one's project or initiative (or well being, success...)

4. Finish by a **clear ask**.

The objective at the end is really to maintain an empathic relationship. This is another key aspect of NVC. Starting with clear observable facts, and expressing our feelings and unfulfilled (or fulfilled) needs, we need to end with a specific ask. An ask could be as simple as "How do you feel about what I just said?" One could also ask how the person has received the feedback by asking her to repeat what she has just heard.

Let's have a look at one example and notice the difference between both feedbacks below. Imagine you are receiving that feedback from your own manager:

Feedback A:
« John , you really need to be more visible! You should really communicate a lot more!» (ok, thanks, that was useful !)

Feedback B:
"John, when you won that sales deal by clearly demonstrating innovation and "a no lose" mentality with Customer Z, but you did not submit a Best Practice/Article/Summary/White paper, I felt a bit frustrated and disappointed. As I shared already, we are building a new culture in our company as well as in our team, and doing so would be very important as I really have the need for the team to be contributing? May I ask you how you feel when I say that?"
John: "Yes, I am comfortable with that"
"May I then ask you to write a one-page summary of what allowed us to win, and submit it to me for review by next Monday?"

Do you feel the difference?
Developing inclusion and empathy in the workspace is possible. Non-judgmental feedback does indeed go a long way in contributing to make our workplace a better place.

The even more difficult art of receiving feedback

After we looked at how NVC can be so helpful in providing constructive and mindful feedback, I would like to discuss how it could also be used when receiving feedback. In the corporate world, managers are taught on giving feedback. But very little is said about receiving feedback.

I believe it is equally important for ecological leaders to be able to receive feedback in a way that really serves them. Let's see why.

Why is it so difficult to receive and hear a feedback?

In other words, why do we tend to hear a critic when we receive a "negative" feedback?

This often comes from the fact that the given feedback is perceived as questioning our very own identity, even sometime as a personal aggression, and not really as they should be, a fresh perspective or development opportunity.

And even when the feedback is specific enough, addresses behaviors, and is expressed in the context of the giver's own needs and feelings.

Our self-esteem is just not strong enough to hear that feedback for what it is: an invitation to grow, peacefully observed with detachment.

Two things here. Generally speaking, it is hard for human beings to accept another person in her difference. And this difference can be conveyed through a feedback that expresses a different opinion or perspective than ours, for instance.

70

The other person will express her difference through a feedback, which, by the way, can be (or not) formulated appropriately, or has been (or not) requested.

Because as a child we have not learned to accept other people's difference (parental or societal conditioning...), it is extremely difficult as adult to accept the difference seen in and heard from others.

In addition, many have grown addicted to how others view and see them. That is why a perceived « negative » feedback can be so devastating. We have developed that addiction in our childhood, and it keeps us fettered. We are begging for our own identity's confirmation by conforming to others' expectations. Thus, through our education, we learned to « buy » someone else's love and appreciation: the love and appreciation of our parents, family, teachers, and then later, our bosses, colleagues, …

A « negative » feedback may deeply shake one's identity while a « positive » feedback will reinforce it.

What to do then when we receive a feedback?

We saw earlier that we have four ways to receive a message and respond to a stimulus. And it is our choice, every moment.

Let's look first at how the SARA model can be really helpful here. SARA is an acronym that we often use to portray the relatively predictable pattern of emotional responses that people feel when an event happens to them that they are not expecting, or when they receive disconfirming feedback. What does it stand for?

- S: shock or surprise

- A: anger or anxiety
- R: rejection or rationalization
- A: acceptance

The 4 steps represent the emotions every person will go through after he receives a difficult feedback as an example. The speed at which one moves from one stage to another varies from person to person, and depends on how the feedback is perceived.

Shock: Our initial response to feedback may be shock, or denial of the feedback, especially if what we hear is unexpected or contradicts our own views. When people are experiencing shock, they may say things like, "This report must not be right," or "What? I don't understand this report."

Anger: As we realize what the feedback means, shock can turn into anger or anxiety, particularly as we see the implications of it. During the anger stage, people may say things like, "Who said this anyway?!" or "This report just doesn't fit my current situation." It can take time until anger disappears.

Resistance: If feedback indicates the need for change, we may experience a period of resistance. Change can be difficult, or at least uncomfortable. When experiencing resistance, people may say, "That's just the way I am, take it or leave it," or "I get it, but I don't like it." They may get stuck in that stage. Sometimes, their level of dissatisfaction and discomfort will get them move and overcome old habits.

Acceptance: Finally, as we process the feedback, we come to a point of acceptance, which leaves us at a higher place than where we started. When an individual is finally accepting their feedback, you may hear them say, "What can I do to improve?" or "How can I best use this feedback?" This is where renewal happens, and people start to project themselves in the future, and consider what they need to get there.

This is why it is so important to be attuned to our feelings and emotions as we receive a feedback. And be aware of the stage we are in.
That self-awareness will tell us what is alive within us, and allows us to choose the best response. Preferably, as we saw earlier, empathy or self-empathy.
This inner clarity will indicate whether our needs for growth, understanding, respect for instance have been met, and if not, will give us the opportunity to clarify with the other person.

« Every feedback is a gift! »

This is what we often hear or say, isn't? Yes, very often the feedback will be useful, and we will indeed benefit from it. But not all feedback is serving us directly. Keep in mind that a feedback is given by another human being… who has his own needs …that he tries to meet through his feedback! That person may very well expresses something which matters to her, and which, very often, corresponds to her own needs. In other words, she is giving a feedback wearing her own glasses. And that is true even when the feedback is well formulated.

When in doubt, it might be worth to clarify by empathizing with the person. I am clearly not saying here you should not listen to any feedback. Just be mindful about the possible distortion caused by where the feedback might be coming form: a place of unmet needs.

Towards more productive meetings

Let's now look at another important aspect of our work lives: meetings. And more specifically, how we can make the most of it.
Given the time we spent in meetings, here is a very simple question: Why are we rarely fulfilled and fully satisfied with their outcome?

Again, keeping it simple and basic on purpose, if we think about it, meetings are gathering of human beings in which we seek to achieve something together: a decision, a common understanding, a plan, strategy, alignment, motivation about an inspiring goal, a review, an assessment,

Therefore, meetings are all great opportunities to stimulate our creativity, bring the best of our talent and fulfill many human needs we all share: collaboration, inclusion, connection, contribution, effectiveness, joy, etc., etc. …

That is where Nonviolent Communication can be so helpful in contributing to more effective, productive, fulfilling and conscious meetings. I have found there are four specific ways that, when put in practice, can change the entire dynamic of your meetings, and consequently, their outcome.

Intention

When we decide to speak in meetings, ask yourself this very simple question: what is my intention behind the words I am about to pronounce? Genuinely? What is the need of mine that I will be fulfilling? Does that really come from a place where I want to help the team to find a solution? Or is it a strategy I use to be heard or seen?

By the way, no judgment here, both are fine in that they serve our needs. But for more productive meetings, checking our intention is a great place to start!

Attention to our own need

Being aware of our needs that are not fulfilled is important. And the good news is that we have very strong cues that we can use: our feelings! Feelings are like warnings on our internal instrument board. If you get bored, exasperated or angry, that is a pretty strong indication your needs are not really fulfilled in the present moment.

Either you can live with that (and having welcomed and brought your feelings and needs to the surface will most certainly start to bring calm). Or you have the courage to express your dissatisfaction and discomfort and your willingness to collectively contribute to a more productive meeting. And that is our choice and responsibility, every moment!

Imagine for a minute that you say instead: "I am sorry to interrupt you but we started our meeting 20 minutes ago, and we still have not started to discuss what we had on the agenda (*Observation*) ; and I am frustrated (*Feeling*) because I need to ensure I use my time appropriately (*Need*) given my current workload. Would you be kind enough to tell me how you currently feel about our meeting as well? (*Ask*)"

That may seem weird at first, or uncomfortable, but you would be surprised by how that will positively change meetings' dynamic and energy.

Attention to the needs of others

75

Our time together is precious, and meetings should not be wasted deciding who is right and who is wrong. If the purpose of the meeting is, for instance, to decide something that everyone should be comfortable with and ready to execute on, it is crucial everyone's needs have been taken in consideration. It does not necessarily mean there will be a consensus about that decision, but the meetings should be held in a way that the needs of the participant are heard. It could be the need to contribute, to be creative, be respected, …

Clear ask

Nonviolent Communication suggests to finish with a clear ask, as this keeps the dialog alive and shows we care about the quality of the communication. Asks should be expressed in present, and should be positive, realistic, attainable and negotiable. At work, I have found that they are really two types of asks you can finish your sentences with:

1. Towards an action.
For instance: "John, would you then be ok to send me your presentation by Monday noon?"

2. Feedback
Here, you will ask either what you said has been understood by for instance asking: "Dave, would you be kind enough to tell me what you have just heard me say?"
Or you can inquire about how he/she feels about what you have just said or asked. For instance: "Helen, may I ask you how you feel after you have heard what I just asked/said?"

Nonviolent Communication can be so helpful in having more productive meetings. And because our needs will most likely be met, the follow-up actions will be taken more enthusiastically. Meetings are truly unique opportunities to develop more ecological connections with each other, and as a result, stronger commitment.

Tune to your own needs and values

We will have spent about 40% of our time in life working by the time we retire. That's a lot, isn't?
Ideally, we all would like our jobs to be as fulfilling and meaningful as possible.
I once came across an interesting article online. It was about the only "acceptable" reason to quit your job, while listing many wrong "reasons" why you should consider instead not quitting your job. Things like "if you feel underpaid", "undervalued", "not challenged enough", "when your values are out of alignment", "when the environment (boss, organization, culture…) no longer fits", "work/life balance feels out of alignment", etc., etc.…

Many of us tend to expect a lot of our work. In other words, using Nonviolent Communication terminology and framework, we expect our jobs to fulfill most (if not all) of our needs!
And that is a lot to ask from our job, employers, boss and/or colleagues don't you think?
The result is that sometimes when we feel incomplete or dissatisfied by our lives, we will blame it on our job and employers! We expect our jobs to be the sole source of expressing our creativity, of fulfilling our needs for connection, spirituality, purpose, and material abundance…

And we all know what expectations produce most of the time as they all share one common attribute: they are rarely met … and create frustration and disappointment!

With NVC, we can gain greater clarity about our needs that are fulfilled at work, and those that are not. Getting clear on our values and needs (which may take months, sometimes years) will in turn lower the expectations you have of your job to fulfill all of them. I reckon that saying "lower our expectations" may sound uninspiring, but the reality is that being clear about those needs and values that are genuinely fulfilled at work and those that are not will bring you peace. You will start to be grateful for what your job caters for. It may even be something you have always taken for granted (for instance, provide material means so that you can live your passion outside of work, or spend quality time with your family).

And more importantly, you will then be able to start looking for strategies to fulfill the needs that are NOT met at work.

Let me use an example. Understanding that your need for creativity is not met, but that your job is great for you to have a social life, human bond or fun, you will accept that your job is not necessarily the most joyful and endless source of happiness for everything in your life (by the way, it may well be!), but already addresses important needs. And then, you start looking at how else you could express your inner creativity.

And that inner understanding and clarity will make you a lot more satisfied at work! As a leader, it will also ensure you are at ease with what you expect from your work. That form of self-awareness will have direct impact on those working around you as you will not project unnecessary expectations onto others.

The same awareness you develop for yourself can then be turned to your team members as well, paying attention to which needs they meet by doing what they do and how they meet them.

From enemy images to empathic inclusion

We have discussed in the previous chapter emerging governance models which can foster more inclusion in our workplaces (we will discuss Holacracy more specifically in the next). In addition to designing organizations in a specific way, we also need to look at how we can personally develop more inclusive attitudes towards our colleagues and bosses.

Marshall Rosenberg described the process of labeling and judging others the "enemy image" process. We have an enemy image whenever we have a judgment, diagnosis, or analysis of someone else or ourselves. At work, that could things like:

"He is not getting it"
"He just can not look at the bigger picture"
"The Marketing guys are not getting it"
"I just do not like the way he always tries to brag about insignificant achievements"
I am sure you can come up with tens of your own examples! And it is important we start to act more inclusively and ecologically as those judgments put static labels on people and keep us separated.

How can we then move from having those enemy images to more inclusive and empathic images? Well, it is pretty similar to what we discussed in the NVC introduction. The process can be simply described in 3 steps:

1. The first step is awareness: realizing that I have such judgments.
2. The idea behind the enemy image process is that if I'm having a judgment, it is an expression of unmet needs. In doing this process, I shift to evaluating whether my needs are met or not. If I can translate the judgment into unmet needs, I will have tapped into the power of the mind, once directed to what is desired, to diligently search for strategies that will meet my needs.
3. If I'm having a judgment of somebody else, then I practice silent empathy, which shifts the focus of my attention onto the needs of the other person by guessing what needs they might be seeking to meet by the conduct that I am judging. I do not have to be "right" about my guesses; the important thing is that I focus my attention on their needs as the motivation for their conduct. I am satisfied with this part of the process when I feel a certain resonance with my guess.

That process which happens in silent allows us to shift from judgment to empathic understanding and connection. From that place, energy between us can flow again as the labels I have put on them are now removed. It does not mean I have to agree with his conduct, but I can now have more constructive conversations in order to find win-win strategies. That process is very ecological by nature as it clears the path towards more authentic relationships. From which can emerge connection rather than anger, resentment or jealousy.

As a manager, being aware of the images we have about people in our teams is a first step. If we keep those images in our heads, they will form micro signals which people will perceive at an unconscious level.

For instance, you may construct enemy images about someone in your team struggling to get a particular task or project done within the timeframe and with the quality you had expected. You had anticipated a particular outcome as you may have, say, 10 years of experience already of dealing with that type of projects. Going through the process:

1. Be aware of the judgments you have ("He is too slow", or "I would have done it already") and your feelings (impatience, possibly frustration...).
2. Self-empathy: what are you unmet needs? Efficiency, personal recognition, contribution?
3. Silent empathy: what are the needs of the other person? Support? Connection? Growth through learning?

A colleague of mine once came to me after he had read on my blog several posts on "Nonviolent Communication" and asked me how he could become more at peace with the images he kept creating.

One of his team colleague kept boasting about his contribution to a team project, and was, according to my colleague, blatantly lying in front of their boss and other team members. He was even challenging others' lack of involvement!

His attitude was generating a great deal of anger and frustration my colleague was struggling to deal with. He was aware of the fact that he was sending silent negative micro-signals. And because that could have rapidly transformed into an endless self-feeding process, he realized he was starting to become violent, both with the other person and with himself.

Reflecting on himself, he also realized he was very often acting as a "White Knight" wanting to bring justice! He had many similar examples of past situations where he simply could not stand the lies of others and where he would systematically seek to expose them as liars.

Together, we went through the process. He was already fully aware of the judgments he was making about the other person.

- First, I invited him to put his feelings into words. Putting feelings into words is important as it allows letting the internal pressure off, and make room for empathy and self-empathy. And ultimately, for strategies and possible next steps. He very quickly identified anger, hostility and animosity towards his colleague. He was also able to express the judgments and feelings he had for himself: he was feeling discouraged, torn, even ashamed for feeling what he was feeling, and not being able to control or transform it.

- We then looked at the unmet needs exposed by the violent feelings he had towards himself and the other person. Mutuality, integrity, trust and respect.

- The third step, which at first was rather challenging, was to guess the other person's feelings and needs. He was possibly feeling insecure, stressed, discouraged. His needs of being seen and understood, needs of support, possibly of security were not satisfied. That helped my colleague to understand that the person's behaviors were driven by very specific human needs. And that he was most certainly adopting certain behaviors as ways of dealing with his unmet needs.

- Going through this process had a number of benefits. Most importantly, it started to bring peace and clarity. The enemy image did not disappear immediately, but I simply invited him to go through the process again every time he felt he would need it. He started to consider the possibility to speak to that person, expressing his own feelings and needs. He also realized he had shut himself down and ignored alternative ways of collaborating with his colleague.

That simple process will allow you to reestablish more authentic relationships. Inclusive of your own needs as well as others'.

Strengths - Cultivate your Unique Brilliance

Now that you have started to pay more attention to your feelings and needs, and use NVC to be a stronger and more authentic communicator, we can learn to maximize our strengths. So that every day at work, you can leverage your unique brilliance and be at your best.

For many years, the conventional wisdom was really about addressing people's so-called weaknesses.

"You need to be better at influencing your peers"

"You need to address a couple of weaknesses I witnessed recently, such as better facilitating meetings"

Annual performance meetings have sometimes been exclusively about elaborating specific development plans to work around team members' "weaknesses".

Well, with the advent of the positive psychology field, it is now recognized that you are much better off maximizing your strengths as opposed to "working" on your weaknesses !

Thus, Seligman and Csikszentmihalyi (2000) charged psychology as a field to understand and document "what work settings support the greatest satisfaction among workers." In response to this challenge, the discipline of positive psychology emerged as an attempt to change the preoccupation with "repairing the worst things in life" into "building positive qualities" (Seligman & Csikszentmihalyi). Positive psychology studies the strengths and virtues that enable individuals and communities to thrive (Bakker & Schaufeli, 2008).

In addition to that, research has also shown that one of the top characteristics of the best teams in organizations out there are teams where members can "use their strengths every day at work".

In other words, start being aware of what gets you excited, when things are easy, effortless and yet very rewarding. Your strengths would be for instance what others say that you have a gift for.

The beauty is that the more you spent on maximizing and developing your strengths, the more fulfilled you feel, and the more successful you will ultimately be.

I had the opportunity to become a certified internal coach at a company I have been working for. Because some of us were already certified coaches, we got trained on a strength-based coaching methodology (based on the Standout assessment, from Markus Buckingham at tmbc.com). We learned to reflect, together with our internal clients, on their strengths, what it meant to them. But more importantly, once that awareness was gained, we worked with them on what to do about it as they were thinking about their next missions, projects or initiatives. I found it fascinating to see how some just transformed themselves as they turned their back to the tyranny of their so-called weaknesses, and choose to focus instead on increasingly leveraging their strengths.

In that process, the first step is to recognize your strengths. Therefore, the prerequisite was for each internal client to go through the Standout assessment (https://www.tmbc.com/).
There are several great personality assessments out there today — DiSC, Myers-Briggs, Herrmann Brain Dominance, StrengthsFinder … and all these assessments give you:

- An understanding of "who you are," and how you are wired
- Great language to describe yourself
- Increased self-awareness

The Standout assessment does that too. Its primary application is to evaluate an individual's strength Roles (combinations of dominant patterns of thought, feeling, and behavior that can be productively applied) and then provide targeted development strategies for using those strength Roles at work. Examples of Roles are "Pioneer", "Equalizer", "Creator", Influencer", "Advisor" … The StandOut assessment was designed to:

- Help leaders pinpoint their own strengths to leverage them with their team members.
- Help team members identify their own strengths to use them in their work.

It measures you on 9 strength Roles and reveals your Top 2. Your results:

- Focus less on who you are and more on what you do
- Describe your edge — where you will have a natural advantage over everyone else
- Measure your impact/output more than your input

In a nutshell, StandOut is a situational judgment test which means it asks you what you would do. It gives you a better understanding about how you show up in the world, and as a result, how you are perceived by your colleagues, for instance.

I could experience first hand as an internal certified Standout coach the power of first developing a very strong awareness about one's own strengths, and then strategies to further leverage them in upcoming projects or assignments.
For those who were willing to do something and follow through after they had completed their assessment and received their reports, you could see a shift happening.

The reason I am primarily mentioning the StandOut methodology is simply because I went through it myself as an individual. I also had the privilege to be coached by experienced TMBC coaches, and then became experienced myself at coaching others.

If you cannot do the assessment, or cannot received strength-based coaching, the SIGN framework below would be a good starting point to become clearer about your top strengths.

Success
- When you do it, you feel effective.
- People tell you that you have a gift for this activity

- You have earned prizes or recognition for this activity

Instinct
- Before you do it, you actively look forward to it.
- You find yourself volunteering for this activity
- This activity is a positive "gut reaction" for you

Growth
- While doing it, you feel inquisitive and focused.
- You often find yourself thinking about this activity
- You can't wait to learn more about this activity

Needs
- After you've done it, you feel fulfilled and authentic.
- It's fun to think back on doing this activity
- Doing this activity is one of your greatest satisfaction

In other words, strengths are go-to activities which make you feel strong and energize you, and often help you increase performance and get recognized in promotions.

I hope that you can start to see how transformative those processes could be. Becoming skilled at communicating with clarity, mindful of your own needs and feelings as well as others', seeking more opportunities to excel at work through the use of your strengths, learning new skills to build them even further, and expanding your job to do this more and more ! This would be truly transformational.

And the resulting fabric, built on strong personal foundations can only be ... vibrant!

Which now leads to the third and last section of this chapter, where we will explore your dominant vibration. And the importance of emanating a strong and clear vibration, which will allow you to attract success in your professional life. Sounds interesting?

Dominant vibration

You will have to bear with me as what I am about to share might possibly sounds esoteric at times.
And yet, I have experienced it over and over with the really brilliant leaders I had the chance to work with.
The best way I have found to describe what they have or do that others do not is that they emanate a clear energy and vibration. Before you start shaking your head in disbelief, let me first try to expand on what I mean here.

First, they have usually a very clear conscience of what we discussed earlier, their feelings and needs, as well as a strong awareness of their strengths.
But what I found is that they exude confidence in what they want. As opposed to what they do not want.
And can quickly move to what they really want once they have realized that they may have fallen into the trap of complaining about what they do not want.
Have you ever paid attention to the amount of time we spend about what we do not want ? Or what we do not want others to do or say ? What a waist of energy !

"He should stop doing this or that"
"She would be better off not to involve those guys in the project"

"They really have no clue, …"

Etc, etc …

Ok, but what do you want ? Expressed in a positive and actionable way?

It is interesting to see how we are struggling to really express our desire, what we want to accomplish.

Expressed in positive terms, and without suffering from the lack of it, or the disappointment of not having it yet. Or without wanting it at the expense of someone else's desire or goal.

Our corporate fabrics need to be vibrant so that innovation can flow, and people can unleash their creativity. And for that to happen, we all need to step up and become vibrant too. And we do that when we are totally clear on what we want to accomplish.

When we are, we create a strong and contagious intention. First for ourselves, but then for others too. And this is when we can create followership around us, which is really another way of looking at leadership.

We emanate and exude confidence, others might say that you are focused and determined, and get things done. This is the process of creation. It is like becoming a magnet which attracts success and inspires others to work with you, be with you, and contribute to your success. In fact, the success of everyone involved in the process of creation.

At first, your awareness of what you do not want helps you identify what you do want; you may feel negative emotion, which helps you know that you are focused upon something unwanted. This is the time to shift and bring more clarity on what you want instead. And as you repeat that process over and over, you will little by little create a strong "vibrational" imprint (for the lack of a better word) around you. Your actions, your thoughts and your feelings are all in congruence to make things happen.

The minute you start communicating and "emanating" what you deeply want, situations and relationships at work will change. People will sense that you are not driven by your ego, but instead by the joy of creating, of doing your very best, of getting things done and of collaborating. People will be attracted to you because of your presence, your "substance", your depth, your sense of connection.

I called this chapter" Vibration", and maybe that word did not speak to you when you started reading it. I hope by now that it makes a lot more sense, and that creating the right conditions and environment at our workplace for people to powerfully "vibrate" is something we shall all be aiming at.

Chapter 6
Performance through agile structures

Now that we have seen how we can individually become more vibrant agents of our corporate fabrics, we also need to look at it from an organizational standpoint. What does it take for organizations to also become vibrant and performant "engines" of growth ? Reconciling performance, productivity, innovation and engagement ?

For organizations to be vibrant and agile, we fundamentally need to upgrade our organizations' operating system.

So that we can move, as depicted on the Holacracy website[7], from

Static Job Descriptions to ...	Dynamic roles
Delegated Authority to ...	Distributed Authority
Large Scale Re-orgs to ...	Rapid Iteration
Alignment via Politics to ...	Transparent rules

Today's organizations very rarely empower the people who work in them. Sadly.

They tend to be barriers to the unleashing of our individual and collective full potential, and hence need to evolve; in other words, organization's fabrics need to be upgraded.

We looked in Chapter 4 at the importance of developing a more acute sense of how our organizations are structured and whether they can allow us to make decisions with more speed and autonomy, how power is distributed or not, and the level of accountability exerted throughout the organization.

While there are several new emerging organizational models, one of the most promising and currently documented model is called Holacracy. Holacracy is about having dynamic roles, distributed authority, rapid iteration in how we evolve the structure, and transparent rules.

---

[7] https://www.holacracy.org/

Holacracy

Holacracy is a method of decentralized management and organizational governance in which authority and decision-making are distributed throughout autonomous, self-organizing teams (circles). Alignment is achieved through a hierarchy of nested circles in which each higher circle defines the purpose for its lower circle(s). Decisions are made by consent, that is the absence of objections, rather than by majority vote.

Holacracy was developed by Brian Robertson, who has codified the system in a now open-sourced constitution. It is based heavily on the Dutch system of Sociocracy which has been implemented in companies since the 1960s (and which I touched on in my previous book, Ecological Leadership). Holacracy and its root method Sociocracy have been adopted by organizations in several countries, the most famous being Zappos in the US.

Let's first discuss the key objectives Holacracy sets to address. You'll certainly find yourself nodding your head as these are objectives that nearly every other management system has failed to achieve!

1. Work roles, domains, and accountabilities are clearly defined as well as projects and next action steps.
2. The above are all visible and transparent in real time (usually through a software portal)
3. Process roles are distinct and separate from any other company roles
4. There are distinct rules and processes for how tensions (issues) are resolved.

5.   The system for handling tensions results in things to be expedited addressed ... without tensions and with autonomy and speed

From the Holacracy website (https://www.holacracy.org/), this new operating system is defined as a "a self-management practice for running purpose-driven, responsive companies. By empowering people to make meaningful decisions and drive change, the Holacracy practice unleashes your organization's untapped power to pursue its purpose in the world."

While this sounds very promising, I would like to expand in this chapter on what it means and how this is actually made possible. Before I do that, you should know that I have become a certified Holacracy practitioner. And while there are many organizational consultants out there with greater experience in helping companies evolving their org structure, I think I have been exposed to Holacracy well enough to share my perspective here, and trust you will gain enough insight to at least decide whether Holacracy (or elements of it) can help you upgrade your own fabric.

Let's dive into the four key elements of Holacracy and what makes it both so unique and powerful : job descriptions, delegated authority, rapid iterations and transparent rules.

In Traditional Companies,

•   Job descriptions: each person has exactly one job. Job descriptions are imprecise, rarely updated, and often irrelevant.

- Delegated Authority: managers loosely delegate authority. Ultimately, their decision always trumps others.
- Big Re-Orgs: the org structure is rarely revisited, mandated from the top.
- Office Politics: implicit rules slow down change and favor people "in the know".

With Holacracy,

- Roles: roles are defined around the work, not people, and are updated regularly. People fill several roles.
- Distributed Authority: authority is truly distributed to teams and roles. Decisions are made locally.
- Rapid Iterations: the org structure is regularly updated via small iterations. Every team self-organizes.
- Transparent Rules: everyone is bound by the same rules, CEO included. Rules are visible to all.

The Holacracy website[8] very clearly articulates what is at stake with regards to roles, authority, agility and transparency. I have reproduced their description below as I think they are really useful if you are just getting exposed to Holacracy.

Dynamic Roles Replace Static Job Descriptions

"In most companies each person has exactly one job description. That description is often imprecise, outdated, and irrelevant to their day-to-day work. In Holacracy, people have multiple roles, often on different teams, and those role descriptions

---

[8] https://www.holacracy.org/

are constantly updated by the team actually doing the work. This allows people a lot more freedom to express their creative talents, and the company can take advantage of those skills in a way it couldn't before. Since roles are not directly tied to the people filling them, people can hand-off and pick-up new roles fairly easily. But more than that, it means that when you're filling a role, you're able to energize the work with a level of clarity and awareness most traditional employees don't have.

For example, in football you know to pass to the striker not because you're friends with him, but because he's in the best position to score. Even if you're mad at the person playing the striker position, you'll still pass the ball to that role because the strategy of the game suggests that you should. Similarly, in Holacracy the roles are vested with authority, not the people. This means that the roles and the authorities can be constantly updated without office politics."

Distributed Authority Replaces Delegated Authority

"The agility that Holacracy provides comes directly from truly distributed authority. In traditional organizations, managers loosely delegate authority, but ultimately, their decisions always trump those they manage and everybody knows it. Any initiative outside the norm typically requires the boss' approval, explicitly or implicitly.

In Holacracy, authority is truly distributed and decisions are made locally by the individual closest to the front line. Teams are self-organized: they are given a purpose, but they decide internally how to best reach it. In this way, Holacracy replaces the traditional hierarchy with a series of interconnected but autonomous teams ("circles"). This shift can dramatically increase a company's capacity to adapt to changing conditions. It also allows those companies to have both alignment and agency without the typical pathologies of "leaderless" groups or autocratic micromanagement that slows everything down."

Rapid Iterations Replace Big Re-orgs

"In traditional companies, the org chart gets revamped every few years. These cyclical "reorgs" are an attempt to keep up with the changing environment, but since they only occur every 3 to 5 years, they are almost always out-of-date. In Holacracy, the structure of the organization is updated every month in every circle (i.e. what roles are doing and owning what work or decisions). This evolution happens in frequent incremental steps rather than rare massive changes, and it happens in every team at all levels. Companies powered by Holacracy reorganize themselves as often as necessary to capitalize on a learning opportunity or address a critical problem. This happens in frequent "governance meetings" where roles and processes are revised given what's actually happening in the team."

Transparent Rules Replace Office Politics

"In many companies, things are done a certain way because "that's how we've always done it", and those implicit rules are hard to change. Often no one knows why those rules exist, who decided them, or who can change them. This makes distributing authority almost impossible, because there is no way to ensure that everyone is following the same set of rules.

In Holacracy, authority is distributed not from the leader at the top to a group of people, but to an explicit process defined in detail in a written document: the Holacracy constitution[9]. Everyone is bound by those same rules, even the CEO. The transparency of the rules means that you no longer have to depend on office politics to get things done. With the fundamental rules made accessible to everyone, anyone in the organization can quickly figure out who owns what, the decisions he or she can make, and who to hold accountable for which functions."

The example of Zappos

One of the earliest adopters of Holacracy is a company called Zappos. Zappos is an interesting company in that it is today the largest company to date (2018) to have embraced and implemented Holacracy.

Zappos has been very transparent to publicly share both their successes and challenges on their journey to implementing self-managed teams and Holacracy. Their CEO, Tony Hsieh, recently reflected on the Holacracy journey at Zappos, in a very enlightening interview with McKinsey[10] . I have decided to reproduce parts of the interview (full link to the McKinsey website in the footnote) as I believe companies like Zappos, despite the bumps they are facing and will continue to face, are paving the way for the future of our organizations.

In terms of corporate structure, what do you think you give up by optimizing for adaptability instead of predictability?

---

[9] https://www.holacracy.org/constitution

[10]   https://www.mckinsey.com/business-functions/organization/our-insights/safe-enough-to-try-an-interview-with-zappos-ceo-tony-hsieh

"Tony Hsieh: There's a quote attributed to Charles Darwin—it may be misattributed—but it's something like, "It's not the fastest or strongest or most intelligent of species that survives. It's the one most adaptable to change." The world is moving faster and faster. Technology is enabling things to happen more and more quickly, and information flows much more quickly than it did 20 to 30 years ago. It's really going from a mind-set of, "How do we try to predict, plan, and control and execute on a specific plan?" to a mind-set that's more about, "How can we get fast feedback loops? How do we constantly sense and respond and build the organization around adaptability and resilience and longevity?" versus the more traditional mind-set of efficiency. (...)

It may be that, on a meta-level, what's less predictable is what our org chart is going to look like six months from now. But I don't know whether predictability is actually an advantage. I think that's how organizations get stuck, because they want that predictability of structure. But if it's the wrong structure, what's the benefit of being predictably wrong? The structure of the organization is a variable that affects the productivity and output of the organization. And most organizations aren't designed for changing their org structure in any efficient or easy way.(...)

We believe that employees are much more than just what their specific job description is. Maybe it's through volunteering at an event, or at the company all-hands meetings where an employee that's great at dancing can go do that even though that has nothing to do with their job description. But beyond just the hobby aspect, I think there's so much creative potential and intelligence that each individual employee has. We're trying to figure out how to create the best structure that releases as much of that as possible. Most structures just end up constraining, so you end up getting 10 percent of a person's potential versus, hopefully, close to 100 percent."

Tony Hsieh's perspective on Holacracy, as a new organizational operating system, is about being able to strike that balance between agility, adaptability and efficiency, and about bringing each and everyone's wholeness at work.

Decision Making Process

One of the best way to ensure everyone gets to be both powerful and successful in what they do is to have a more inspiring decision-making process.

As Frederic Laloux describes it in his book "Reinventing Organizations", the pyramidal structures hinder fast and effective decision making. And does not always create the necessary level of engagement for decisions to be implemented swiftly.

"In a pyramid structure, meetings are needed at every level to gather, package, filter, and transmit information as it flows up and down the chain of command. In self-managing structures, the need for these meetings falls away almost entirely. Meeting overload in traditional organizations is particularly acute the higher you go up the hierarchy.

Decisions are naturally pushed up to the top, as it's the only place where decisions and trade-offs can be informed from the various angles involved. It's almost deterministic: with a pyramidal shape, people at the top of organizations will complain about meeting overload, while people below feel disempowered.”

We often think that decisions can be made in only two general ways: either through hierarchical authority (someone calls the shots; many people might be frustrated, but at least things get done) or through consensus (everyone gets a say, but it's often frustratingly slow and sometimes things get bogged down because no consensus can be reached).
Sadly, this is what we see all too often:

> *"Consensus comes with another flaw. It dilutes responsibility. In many cases, nobody feels responsible for the final decision. The original proposer is often frustrated that the group watered down her idea beyond recognition; she might well be the last one to champion the decision made by the group. For that reason, many decisions never get implemented, or are done so only half-heartedly. If things don't work out as planned, it's unclear who is responsible for stepping in.”*

Frederic Laloux's book gives several examples of successful implementations of more powerful decision-making processes. For instance, here is how decisions are made at Buurtzorg, one of his researched companies.

> *"Buurtzorg teams use a very precise and efficient method for joint problem solving and decision-making. The group first chooses a facilitator for the meeting. The agenda of topics to be discussed is put together on the spot, based on what is present for team members at that moment in time. The facilitator is not to make any statements, suggestions, or*

decisions; she can only ask questions: "What is your proposal?" or "What is the rationale for your proposal?" All proposals are listed on a flipchart. In a second round, proposals are reviewed, improved, and refined. In a third round, proposals are put to a group decision. The basis for decision-making is not consensus. For a solution to be adopted, it is enough that nobody has a principled objection. A person cannot veto a decision because she feels another solution (for example, hers!) would have been preferable. The perfect solution that all would embrace wholeheartedly might not exist, and its pursuit could prove exhausting. As long as there is no principled objection, a solution will be adopted, with the understanding that it can be revisited at any time when new information is available."

Clearly, one of Holacracy's strength is that it truly fosters a much higher level of agility throughout the company fabric.

The way decision making happens contributes to it tremendously. The decision making process is inclusive by design, and brings immediate benefits in team's participation and engagement. This is at the heart of Holacracy and other dynamic governance models available out there.

At a high level, the process can be described as follows:

1. Identify what exactly needs to be decided and acted upon
2. Propose a solution to address a specific tension
3. Consent to the proposal

    a. Present proposal
    b. Clarifying round – clarifying questions only

c. Quick reaction round – quick feedback about the proposal; as appropriate, (optionally) amend the proposal based on the reactions/questions.

d. Consent round – if objections, record on a flip chart without dialog until the round is completed; if necessary, amend proposal and repeat consent round. (If needed, a dialog may be initiated until potential amendments begin to emerge.)

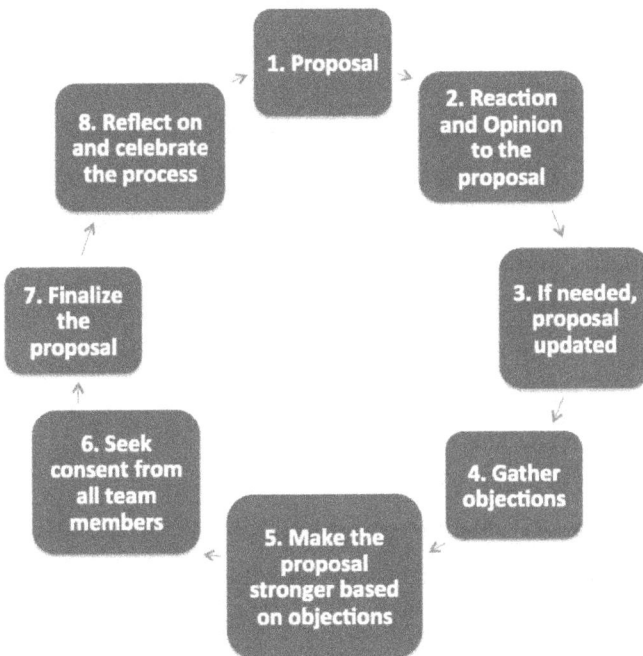

We discussed earlier the difference between consent and consensus. It can be difficult at first to challenge how we have made decisions for so long, but with practice and experienced facilitators, you will notice how faster and more empowering the whole process becomes.

Distributed Power

All we have seen in our corporate lives are hierarchical pyramids and this is really all we have known as organizational structures.

When we look at the topic of distributed power, the question is less about "how can everyone have equal power?", but rather "how can everyone be powerful?". Power is not viewed as a zero-sum game, where the power I have is necessarily power taken away from you. The devastating effect of this unequal power distribution is all to well known : very little engagement, stifled innovation and creativity. Personal ambition, politics, mistrust. And resentment. What a waist of energy and talent!

In an attempt to address some of these issues, several companies have started to follow an advice process to restore a more equal distribution of power.

For instance, a project manager will have to seek the advice of as many stakeholders as possible to come to the best proposal (and later, decision) possible. Even the CEO can be one of the many consulted persons. The process is key to making self-management work on a large scale. People "higher up" cannot simply overrule these decisions based on hierarchical position, because they are « simply » one of the many stakeholders whose opinion is sought. Sure, a CEO's opinion may have bigger weight given his experience and position, but still, he would "only" be one of many. And he would have no power to revert decisions made through the advice process.

Contrast it with consensus seeking! With the advice process, the ownership for the decision stays clearly with one person: the decision maker. While consensus drains energy out of organizations, the advice process boosts motivation and initiative.

Let's have a look at it the benefits of the advice process as described in Frederic Laloux's book, "Reinventing Organizations".

> *"First, it draws people whose advice is sought into the question at hand. They learn about the issues and become knowledgeable critics or cheerleaders. The sharing of information reinforces the feeling of community. Each person whose advice is sought feels honored and needed.*
>
> *Second, asking for advice is an act of humility, which is one of the most important characteristics of a fun workplace. The act alone says, "I need you." The decision maker and the adviser are pushed into a closer relationship. In my experience, this makes it nearly impossible for the decision maker to simply ignore advice.*
>
> *Third, making decisions is on-the-job education. Advice comes from people who have an understanding of the situation and care about the outcome. No other form of education or training can match this real-time experience.*
>
> *Fourth, chances of reaching the best decision are greater than under conventional top-down approaches. The decision maker has the advantage of being closer to the issue and ... usually has to live with the consequences of the decision.*
>
> *Fifth, the process is just plain fun for the decision maker because it mirrors the joy found in playing team sports. ... The advice process stimulates initiative and creativity, which are enhanced by wisdom from knowledgeable people elsewhere in the organization"*

Ensuring everyone gets to be powerful is, I believe, one of the key success factor that can explain the spectacular outcomes of the pioneer organizations researched in the book "Reinventing Organizations". What we are really talking about is the need to create an empowering fabric.

I remember an interesting discussion I had with a coworker a while back when visiting a branch office at a company I worked for. They had just lost their local leader, and that individual said to me : "Who will be in charge now ?" That question (a statement, really) stuck with me as I found interesting we can sometimes be quick to adopt the victim's stance, and feel disempowered !

I actually happened to personally know that leader, and he would be the first to tell you that he genuinely intended to empower his teams. So, why is that, that despite his genuine intention, some would still quickly fall back to the victim's stance. I think it has a lot to do with the fabric itself. If you have a "disempowering fabric", regardless of what the leader at the top will say or do, he will end up playing the role of the hero, and team members, that of the victim. The intentions (and behaviors) of that leader were totally genuine, but somehow, they were not "creating" powerful and empowered teams.

This is where we need a fabric with the right structures and processes to empower everyone. As an example, Holacracy ensures a space is hold for everyone to use their power to the level they need to be successful. Like in the advice process discussed above, not even the leader can dominate others with his power.

As a result, we no longer need to rely on leaders to empower us. Instead we have something much more powerful: a fabric in which we can all develop our own empowerment in service of a larger purpose and all act as leaders.

Concretely, this requires a new power structure for the organization, and new processes which hold and distribute authority.

Ironically, this will take leaders who empower a system to empower others, by heroically and permanently releasing their authority!

Let me quote again Tony Hsieh, CEO at Zappos, from the same interview he did with McKinsey:

"If a company is self-organizing, and being dependent on a CEO can be considered a point of failure, how does the company keep its bearings?

"Tony Hsieh: Cities are another example of self-organization. Cities are the man-made organizations that have best stood the test of time. Cities last much longer than companies. Cities are resilient. Cities are adaptable. And cities aren't hierarchical the way most companies are. (...)

Not only do cities stand the test of time, there's plenty of evidence they actually scale in terms of productivity and innovation. One interesting statistic is that whenever the size of a city doubles, innovation or productivity per resident increases 15 percent. But in companies you get the opposite effect. As companies get bigger, they usually get more bureaucratic and less innovative per employee. The mayor of a city doesn't tell its residents what to do or where to live; there is a certain infrastructure that a city must provide, such as the grid: water, power, and sewage. And there are certain basic laws that a city enforces. But for the most part, what happens when a city grows and innovates is a result of the self-organization that happens with a city's residents, businesses, and other organizations."

Accountability

In Chapter 4, we looked at an organization's level of accountability as a strong indicator of a fabric's organizational "health".

As Brian Robertson, founder of Holacracy, puts it in his blog[11] "If it's not explicit, no one has a right to expect it"

"To make these once-healthy behaviors no longer useful, we must first remove the implicit expectation that others should align with our implicit expectations (or anyone else's). This requires an effective governance process – one which itself is documented explicitly, not wielded implicitly (e.g. captured in a written Constitution[12]). The Holacracy governance process generates clarity by defining explicit roles[13] with explicit accountabilities, which grant explicit authority, and continuously evolving these to integrate learning and align with the organization's ever-changing reality. This removes power from the implicit norms and instead vests power in an explicit process[14], and the expectations and authorities which result. (...)

For us humans, this shift has a fascinating effect on the culture and personal relationships at play, and one I find incredibly liberating – our personal relationships are freed from being used (or abused) to navigate or enforce implicit expectations or persuade others of their merit. Our relationships become different from – or rather, differentiated from – the organizational drama and the needs

---

[11] https://blog.holacracy.org/obsoleting-organizational-politics-2f4627d557d4

[12] https://www.holacracy.org/constitution

[13] https://blog.holacracy.org/differentiating-role-and-soul-fe8cf5d53cc1

[14] https://blog.holacracy.org/the-power-of-governance-680a2a6bcc22

of the work. Good explicit governance gets those things out of the way, and allows us to hold whatever personal relationships we choose to build as sacred, beyond the reach of organizational pressures and politics."

Holacracy makes it all more explicit, transparent, and as result, creates the space in which people will thrive by raising their personal level of accountability.
Once people start to be fully accountable and empowered, they will "naturally" detect, and act upon the tensions they sense within the organization, and process it into positive change, one tension at a time.

As Brian Robertson describes it, *"Holacracy's approach is first to shift the top-down power structure to a distributed control system embedded within a fractal structure, one which allows self-organization at every level of scale, so most tensions can be processed locally.*

That mindset change, one that elevates people to empowered "sensors" and leaders who know they can make a difference at their level, is well illustrated by Tony Hsieh's at Zappos.

"One of the learnings we've had about self-organization and self-management is that it's not just a systems change; it's also a personal journey for each individual employee. Self-organization and self-management is about the entrepreneurial mind-set. A study was done several years ago that looked at what separated the great entrepreneurs from the mediocre ones. They found that the great entrepreneurs highly overindex for three characteristics: first, being comfortable with ambiguity; second, having a strong sense of curiosity; and third—not as high, but still overindexed—was

emotional intelligence. And I think under self-organization, these three characteristics are even more important for us to hire for at Zappos.

To harness collective intelligence, we think of every single employee as a human sensor. Everyone senses different things, and you want a way to process all of that input. An airplane is one analogy. There are all of these different sensors. Some sensors, like the altimeter, are probably more important than others, but you want to be aware of all of them. Even if the altimeter looks fine, and most of the other sensors look fine, that doesn't mean it's OK to ignore the low-voltage warning light when it turns on. You don't allow the other sensors to outvote the low-voltage warning light and ignore it, yet the analogous thing happens all the time in organizations."

Common misconceptions

Because self-management and organizational models such as Holacracy , while gaining great traction, are still relatively new. And have also met their fair share of active resistance as well as misperception and objections. That is why I choose to close this chapter by looking at the most commonly heard misperceptions about self-management.

In this chapter, I choose to partially keep the original article and reproduce it almost entirely (the link to its public URL in the footnote) as I believe hearing directly from the author of "Reinventing Organization" and the founder of Holacracy gives additional perspective on the kind of the paradigm shift we will need to embrace in the coming years.

It is actually "healthy" to see those critiques and misperceptions as they give more opportunities to address them and explain the shift we collectively need to operate. All we have known for several decades are hierarchical structures, and therefore it will take time for leaders to 1. be willing to be receptive to new models and 2. start to embrace them through pilots and experiments.

Frederic Laloux's article[15] addresses 4 misconceptions on self-management, of which I have reproduced the first 3 as they seemed to be more fitting in the context of what we discussed in the chapter.

Misperception 1: There is no structure, no management, no leadership

"People who are new to the idea of Self-Management sometimes mistakenly assume that it simply means taking the hierarchy out of an organization and running everything democratically based on consensus. There is, of course, much more to it. Self-Management, just like the traditional pyramidal model it replaces, works with an interlocking set of structures, processes, and practices; these inform how teams are set up, how decisions get made, how roles are defined and distributed, how salaries are set, how people are recruited or dismissed, and so on.

What often puzzles us at first about self-managing organizations is that they are not structured along the control-minded hierarchical templates of Newtonian science. They are complex, participatory, interconnected, interdependent, and continually evolving systems, like ecosystems in nature. Form follows need. Roles are picked up, discarded, and exchanged fluidly. Power is distributed. Decisions are made at the point of origin. Innovations

[15] http://www.self-managementinstitute.org/misperceptions-of-self-management

111

can spring up from all quarters. Meetings are held when they are needed. Temporary task forces are created spontaneously and quickly disbanded again. (...)

The tasks of management—setting direction and objectives, planning, directing, controlling, and evaluating—haven't disappeared. They are simply no longer concentrated in dedicated management roles. Because they are spread widely, not narrowly, it can be argued that there is more management and leadership happening at any time in self-managing organizations despite, or rather precisely because of, the absence of full-time managers."

Misperception 2: Everyone is equal

"For as long as human memory goes back, the problem of power inequality has plagued life in organizations. Much of the pervasive fear that runs silently through organizations—and much of the politics, the silos, the greed, blaming, and resentment that feed on fear—stem from the unequal distribution of power.(...)

Here we stumble upon a beautiful paradox: people can hold different levels of power, and yet everyone can be powerful. If I'm a machine operator—if my background, education, interests, and talents predispose me for such work—my scope of concern will be more limited than yours, if your roles involve coordinating the design of a whole new factory. And yet, if within what matters to me, I can take all necessary actions using the advice process, I have all the power I need.

This paradox cannot be understood with the unspoken metaphor we hold today of organizations as machines. In a machine, a small turn of the big cog at the top can send lots of little cogs spinning. The reverse isn't true—the little cog at the bottom can try as hard as it pleases, but it has little power to move the bigger cog.

112

The metaphor of nature as a complex, self-organizing system can much better accommodate this paradox. In an ecosystem, interconnected organisms thrive without one holding power over another. (...)

It's the same in self-managing organizations: the point is not to make everyone equal; it is to allow all employees to grow into the strongest, healthiest version of themselves. Gone is the dominator hierarchy (the structure where bosses hold power over their subordinates). And precisely for that reason, lots of natural, evolving, overlapping hierarchies can emerge—hierarchies of development, skill, talent, expertise, and recognition, for example."

Misperception 3: It's about empowerment

"Many organizations today claim to be empowering. But note the painful irony in that statement. If employees need to be empowered, it is because the system's very design concentrates power at the top and makes people at the lower rungs essentially powerless, unless leaders are generous enough to share some of their power. In self-managing organizations, people are not empowered by the good graces of other people. Empowerment is baked into the very fabric of the organization, into its structure, processes, and practices. Individuals need not fight for power. They simply have it.

For people experiencing Self-Management for the first time, the ride can be bittersweet at first. With freedom comes responsibility: you can no longer throw problems, harsh decisions, or difficult calls up the hierarchy and let your bosses take care of it. You can't take refuge in blame, apathy, or resentfulness. Everybody needs to grow up and take full responsibility for their thoughts and actions—a steep learning curve for some people. Former leaders and managers sometimes find it is a huge relief not having to deal with

everybody else's problems. But many also feel the phantom pain of
not being able to wield their former positional power.

After looking in Chapter 5 at our personal vibration, we started this
chapter by asking:
 "What does it take for organizations to also become vibrant and
performing "engines" of growth ? Reconciling performance,
productivity, innovation and engagement ? For organizations to be
vibrant and agile?"
We have looked at self-managed and agile structures (and Holacracy
in more details) which, when fully embraced, will produce the kind
of next-generation fabric we need.

Chapter 7
Your leadership

Up until now, we have been looking at the importance of developing stronger personal and organizational awareness. We then looked at how to unleash the full potential of ourselves and of our organizations. As we have seen, this starts inwardly, with an inner introspection and discovery process that allows us to transform ourselves and become more vibrant actors of our organizations' fabric. Similarly, upgrading our organizations's fabric produces a more fertile soil for what needs to emerge. The right foundation for us all to express our leadership, and for our organizations to give room to more innovation.

115

While the last 2 chapters have been about inward transformation, inward "upgrades", leadership and innovation, for instance, are applied outward, towards others, teams and customers... Let's see how leadership can now be fully and authentically expressed!

So much has been written on leadership ! How to become a leader, the difference between leaders and managers, business leaders and people leaders, the required skills of leadership, soft and hard skills of leaders, etc, etc...

The business literature has discussed it at length and will continue to do so. If I were to ask you, you would have your own definition of leadership. You have seen throughout your career many acts of leadership and worked with many great and not so great leaders. And so did I.

Personally, leadership really comes down to those three things:

1. Leaders get things down and get results
2. Leaders are agents of change
3. By inspiring the people they touch through authenticity and trust

You might think : wait a minute, I could add about ten other things to that (short) list !

And those ten additional characteristics would undoubtedly be "right" too!

I am only sharing those 3 things, because they have been my own experience as a leader and in working with many other leaders, at work or outside of work.

What we will really discuss here as we continue our journey, from personal awareness and raising our vibration to leadership, is that, in order to achieve 1. and 2., getting things down and results and driving change, it all starts with 3..

It starts with who you are as a leader, how you indeed inspire others, how you "touch" others and create the space and the opportunity for people you work with to bring their best.

We rarely look at it this way. Instead, we mostly focus on the outcome (dollars, growth, market share wins…) as opposed to the qualities leaders need to embody to get to this results.

What we are saying here is that it starts with your ability to be aware of your inner world, your programming, and from there, to raise your personal vibration, developing a more empathic communication style, tapping into your brilliance repeatedly and become that powerful magnet, attracting what you want, for you and your teams.

This all leads to unfolding your natural leadership, your qualities can then be fully expressed as you become that inspiring leader.

I describe it as going outwards because this unfolding has ripple effects, touching the people you work with (colleagues, partners, customers) and leading to the business results you manifest as a result.

Leadership is about leading from the heart and it is about emanating trust. What I am saying here is that expressing with full confidence and determination your authenticity, leading with trust and from your heart, are what leaders are here to bring to the world.

Sustainable results, performance and growth will only be a consequence of the conditions created by the kind of leadership we will now discuss.

Heart-Based Leadership

The Heart and the Head

Author and teacher Parker Palmer described the 'heart' as "that centre in the human self where everything comes together (where will and intellect and values and feeling and intuition and vision all converge). It meant the source of one's integrity. It takes courage to lead from the heart."

The heart is center of one's personality, the center of character and emotional life. The heart is connected with our intuition and emotion. Our body is our vessel to make things happen, our joy to create, our strength to overcome obstacles. "Heart" drives feelings, emotions, intuitions, actions, and reactions. Therefore, the heart "knows". He knows how best to deal with specific situations, with the complexity of our world. Heart-based leadership takes the whole into account.

Talking to and winning both the head and the heart of organizations and team members is essential in today's world. With the new Millennials joining the workforce, speaking only to their head using managerial and analytical tools will not suffice. Yes, one still needs to be rational, logical and structured as our IQ-type of intelligence is required to form answers to complex issues.

Balancing your head and heart is essential to great leadership. It creates an healthier and more resilient ecology among people, and helps bring a sense of purpose. In other words, the "Why" and" How" things are done are as important as the "What". The values you show and embody as a leader and as a role model matter. The quality of the relationships you build and maintain also matter so that challenges and setback are not excuses to find culprits, but opportunities to grow and learn from. Starting to see people as ... "people" and not as "guys who report to me", "guys who need to play by the rule" or "who are here to deliver XYZ every month" will create unprecedented levels of engagement.

In other words, what if we could ask ourselves that simple question when faced with difficult situations and decisions to make?: "what would my heart think, do and say?"
I am sure there are more, but I have found the 4 heart-based leadership's characteristics below to be the most inspiring and powerful to create sustainable performance.
1.   Serving and developing people
2.   Humility
3.   Empathy
4.   Trust

Serving and developing people

I have read somewhere that the company IBM often said that it did not want to develop 200 or 1000 leaders, but 50000 as that is what they will need in the future.

Whether that is just wishful thinking or real, it does not matter. True leaders need to see their position of influence as great opportunities to genuinely help others to also become leaders. And to serve people has a basic prerequisite: you need to make sure you actually see those you work with as people, not just as "people filling a role". People will play different roles in their lives (father, friend, manager, wife, husband …). In the workplace alone, we do also have many different roles.

119

But those roles do not define who we ultimately are. They do not define our identity. Serving team members and colleagues is therefore going way beyond seeing them as objects to which we devote more or less attention depending on how much they will be useful to us!

This is where nonviolent communication has so much to teach us as we saw earlier. As soon as you realize that human beings have most of their needs in common, people you lead will have the same need for development and growth that you have. Therefore, using your position, clout and skills to help them grow is true leadership. And in turn, they will be much more likely to follow you as a leader and be engaged in their work.

The good news is that you, as a leader, also gets a nice bonus ! Research has shown that, while material happiness provides a little boost, it does not last. In contrast, when we serve and contribute, when there is a connection, contribution and purpose, the sense of happiness we get as a result is more lasting and fulfilling. By stepping across our judgements and reaching out to our common humanity. A leader has tens of opportunities a day to do just that!

Humility

Leading from the heart. Serving and developing your team. This is where humility is needed, and needs to be cultivated. That cannot be done with our ego in the driver seat.
We see leaders stealing credit for those that are underneath them and not protecting them when something goes wrong. We see leaders not making decisions or implementing ideas from other people just because of their own egos.

Interestingly, Jim Collins in his book "Good to Great: Why Some Companies Make the Leap... and Others Don't " discovered what makes companies go from good to great by sifting through massive amount of data.

He started with the set of every company that has appeared on Fortune 500 from 1965 to 1995, and identified companies that started out merely as "good" companies and then became "great" companies (defined as outperforming the general market by a factor of three or more) for an extended period of time (defined as fifteen years or more). He ended up with a set of eleven "good to great" companies and compared them to a set of "comparison companies" to determine what made the merely good companies become great.

Those companies have what Jim Collins describes as Level 5 Leaders: a unique mix of humility and professional will.

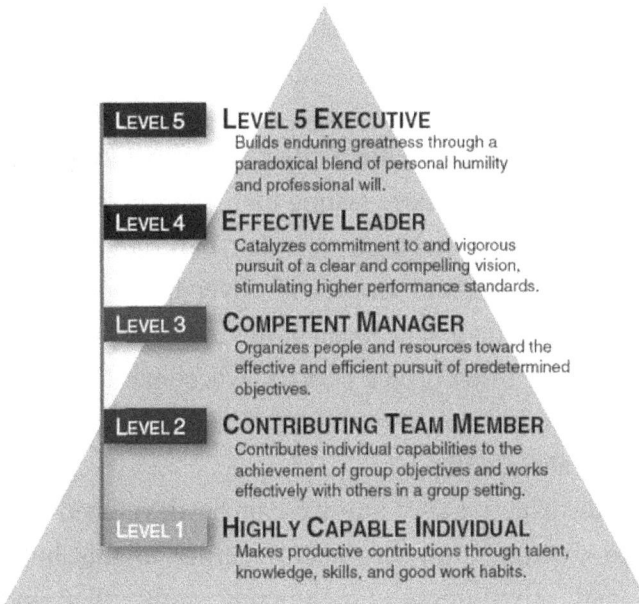

LEVEL 5 — **LEVEL 5 EXECUTIVE**
Builds enduring greatness through a paradoxical blend of personal humility and professional will.

LEVEL 4 — **EFFECTIVE LEADER**
Catalyzes commitment to and vigorous pursuit of a clear and compelling vision, stimulating higher performance standards.

LEVEL 3 — **COMPETENT MANAGER**
Organizes people and resources toward the effective and efficient pursuit of predetermined objectives.

LEVEL 2 — **CONTRIBUTING TEAM MEMBER**
Contributes individual capabilities to the achievement of group objectives and works effectively with others in a group setting.

LEVEL 1 — **HIGHLY CAPABLE INDIVIDUAL**
Makes productive contributions through talent, knowledge, skills, and good work habits.

Here are some key principles of level 5 leaders.

a) "Level 5 leaders embody a paradoxical mix of personal humility and professional will."

121

b) "Level 5 leaders set up their successors for even great success in the next generation, whereas egocentric leaders often set up their successors for failure."

c) "Level 5 leaders are fanatically driven, infected with an incurable need to produce sustained *results*. They are resolved to do whatever it takes."

d) "Level 5 leaders display a workman-like diligence – more plow horse than show horse."

e) "Level 5 leaders look out the window to attribute success to factors other than themselves. When things go poorly, however, they look in the mirror and blame themselves, taking full responsibility."

f) "Level 5 leaders attribute much of their success to good luck, rather than personal greatness."

Some lower-level leaders will struggle to get there. They will never bring themselves to subjugate their own needs to the greater ambition of something larger and more lasting than themselves. Their work will always be first and foremost of what they get – fame, fortune, owner, adulation, etc. And work will never be about what they build, create and contribute. The great irony is that the animus and personal ambition that often drives people to become a Level 4 leader stands at odds with the humility required to rise to Level 5.
How do you then cultivate humility?

In my personal experience, humility can be developed and cultivated. We have discussed several "tools" earlier in this book such as empathy and mindfulness. Empathizing with other and understanding other's needs result into a greater sense of humility. A sense of people being connected, sharing the same needs and the same essence. Great leaders are humble. The mistake would be to assume they are weak because of their humbleness. Ambition, decisiveness and professional can coexist with humility, as show in the "Good to Great" companies.

Empathy

Empathy is the recognition of the feelings and needs of others. The day I realized that we, human beings, have basically the same needs, and that we create conflicts mostly because we simply disagree on our strategies to fulfill those common needs, has been life changing.

As Chade-Meng Tan wrote in his book, "Search inside yourself", *"kindness is the engine of empathy; it motivates you to care, and it makes you more receptive to others, and them to you.*

What we think, we become. The practice of creating mental habits is based on a simple, intuitively obvious yet profoundly important insight. It has been described this way: Whatever one frequently thinks and ponders upon, that will become the inclination of his mind. In other words, what we think, we become. The method itself is simple; invite a thought to arise in your mind often enough, and it will become a mental habit.

For example, if every time you see another person, you wish for that person to be happy, then eventually, your instinctive first thought is to wish for that person to be happy. After a while, you develop an instinct for kindness. You become a kind person. Your kindness shows in your face, posture, and attitude every time you meet somebody. When you project kindness people intuitively trust you. They will sense you have their best interests at heart. Developing a trusting relationship with employees and co-workers is one of the essentials of working in an office.

Even in difficult situations, it is sometimes possible to make important things happen while still creating workplace friendships. It

123

requires a kind heart, an open mind, and the right social skills. When you must have an uncomfortable conversation with someone, instead of avoiding it or approaching it emotionally, use your skills to make the situation a learning experience. If you're unhappy with the performance of a worker, instead of speaking to them in anger, try using kindness. Show you care about their performance and work with them to identify possible avenues for improvement. By offering to work with them, you make your employee feel supported and respected.

One word on compassion. Compassion is a mental state endowed with a sense of concern for the suffering of others and aspiration to see that suffering relieved. The most compelling benefit of compassion in the context of work is that compassion creates highly effective leaders. So how do you become a compassionate leader? The practice of compassion is about going from self to others. In a way, compassion is about going from "I" to "We"

These leaders are highly ambitious, but the focus of their ambition is not themselves; instead, they are ambitious for the greater good. Because their attention is focused on the greater good, they feel no need to inflate their own egos. That makes them highly effective and inspiring.
So instead of focusing on how your team makes you look, focus on how your team can improve as a whole. When you want everyone to succeed, you'll get better results."

And ... Trust ...

As Simon Sinek wrote [16]so nicely in Sept 2016, "When we tell people to do their jobs, we get workers. When we trust people to get the job done, we get leaders."

---

[16] https://www.linkedin.com/pulse/when-we-tell-people-do-jobs-get-workers-trust-

Let's therefore further explore trust-based leadership, the key to unlocking performance and unleashing innovation!

Trust-based Leadership

Data confirms what great leaders knew already!

Let me start by sharing the results of a very interesting project Google led a couple of years ago with the goal to discover the secret to building more productive and stellar teams.

The project, known as Project Aristotle[17], took several years, and included analysis of data about the people on more than 100 active teams at the company.

Google's data-driven approach ended up highlighting what leaders in the business world have known for a while; the best teams respect one another's emotions and are mindful that all members should contribute to conversation equally. It has less to do with who is in a team, and more with how team members interact with one another.

The answer is simple yet profound: it turns out that the secret of teamwork is being kind to people.

Here are a few key components of Google's secret to teamwork:

---

job-done-simon-sinek

[17]   https://www.nytimes.com/2016/02/28/magazine/what-google-learned-from-its-quest-to-build-the-perfect-team.html

Team dynamics are more important than team makeup: Many managers might think that a great team "just happens" if you get the right people with the right skills and personalities in the right jobs. But according to Google's research, the strength of a team has less to do with which people are on the team, and more to do with how the team interacts.

Respect and collaboration: The best teams tend to respect each other's feelings and create safe spaces for open conversation where everyone can feel comfortable contributing. Productive teams are good at making an effort to understand and relate to each other – and this starts with simple respect and open communication.

Psychological safety: Are people on your team comfortable with making themselves vulnerable, sharing what's really on their mind, confiding in each other, and pausing the conversation to ask for clarity? Or is your team more tight-lipped and tense? The best teams cultivate a feeling of "psychological safety," where no one is worried about feeling embarrassed or bullied, and where people feel safe asking questions and proposing the "craziest" ideas. When team members feel safe, accepted, and understood, they are able to feel more comfortable sharing ideas and taking risks.

At the heart of Google's findings, is the concept of "psychological safety[18]", a model of teamwork in which members have a shared belief that it is safe to take risks and share a range of ideas without the fear of being humiliated.

Google now describes psychological safety as the most important factor to building a successful team.

"There were other behaviors that seemed important as well — like making sure teams had clear goals and creating a culture of dependability. But Google's data indicated that psychological safety, more than anything else, was critical to making a team work."

---

[18] https://rework.withgoogle.com/blog/five-keys-to-a-successful-google-team/

In short, just be nice and kind! In the best teams, members listen to one another and show sensitivity to feelings and needs.

According to Google's research, great teamwork is not a matter of talent; it's a matter of creating a safe space for people to practice kindness, respect and empathy for their teammates. Productivity comes from mutual understanding – when people trust their teammates to be on their side, they will be ready to do great things.

However, establishing psychological safety is, by its very nature, somewhat difficult to implement. We will look at how trust-based leadership creates that soil on which effective corporate fabrics can thrive.

The power of trust

More often than not, when companies want to develop a manager or leader, and hope that this will boost their team's productivity and engagement, they will likely send them to some kind of training. This is usually the first response to one's development need.

The challenge is that when it comes to soft skills (such as developing your coaching or listening skills, empathy, facilitation skills, assertiveness...), the longer-term effects of those trainings can sometimes be questioned.

Why? In short, because most of the time these trainings are primarily about fixing things or addressing gaps, but are rarely designed to help trainees fundamentally change their behaviors, their profound way of being and operating in the world. It really takes a sustained effort and resolve for someone to not just change a few aspects of his leadership and/or management style, but to deeply transform himself.

Not only that! Depending on how management higher in the organization sees the world, and because of their own filters, they are likely to identify and recommend the "wrong" gaps to be addressed.

At one point in my career, many years ago, a VP suggested to me that, should I have wanted to further climb the corporate ladder, I needed to display more of the 3 "A": Ambition, Aggression and Assertiveness. Aggression, really?!

Contrast it with Google latest study and findings discussed in the previous section which talks about kindness and providing a "safe environment" for teams to be at their best!

Do we need a new approach to develop managers, and as a result, teams? I believe so.

Only a leader, who, as a human being, will make the conscious effort to evolve from a fear-based to a trust-based perspective and leadership, will have a profound and lasting impact on his teams, and on the business.

As I look for myself, and try to "isolate" the one thing that really allowed me to perform at my best over the years, and I hope, allowed people in my teams to do so too, I indeed can bring it down to trust. Trust is the cement from which all success can be built upon.

Patrick Lencioni's perspective on trust which he shares in his book "The Five Dysfunctions of a Team" is really interesting in that regard. He explains that trust is the essential foundation of highly effective teams (and organizations). As can be seen from the layered pyramid below, lack of trust in the end leads to inattention to results.

"The five dysfunctions" are, in order of causality:

1. Absence of trust: People do not trust the intentions of their teammates. They feel the need to protect themselves from each other and tread carefully around others on the team. This leads to the next dysfunction.

2. Fear of conflict: Without trust, people are unwilling to involve themselves in productive debates and conflicts, the type of good conflict that focuses entirely on resolving issues without involving character attacks or hidden personal agendas. Without such healthy conflicts, issues stay unresolved or are unsatisfactorily resolved. People feel they have not been properly involved in decisions. This leads to the next dysfunction.

3. Lack of commitment: When people feel their input has not been properly considered and that they have not been properly involved in decisions, they have no buy-in. They do not commit to the final decisions. Ambiguity about priorities and directions festers, and uncertainties linger. This leads to the next dysfunction.

4. Avoidance of accountability: When people have no buy in about decisions, they avoid accepting accountability. Worse still, they do not hold their teammates accountable to high standards. Resentment festers, and mediocrity spreads. This leads to the final dysfunction.

5. Inattention to results: The ultimate dysfunction of a team. People care about something other than the collective goals of the team. Goals are not met, results are not achieved.

It all begins with trust. The absence of trust is the root cause of all other dysfunctions. Specifically, the type of trust Lencioni talks about is what he calls "vulnerability-based trust." That is when "team members trust the intentions of each other enough that they are willing to expose their own vulnerabilities because they are confident their exposed vulnerabilities will not be used against them. Hence, they are willing to admit issues and deficiencies and ask for help. In other words, they are able to concentrate their energies on achieving the team's common goals, rather than wasting time trying to defend their egos and look good to their teammates."

I have tried to identify how shifting from a fear-based to a trust-based perspective can be translated in day-to-day situations at work.

Fear-Based	Trust-Based
Be visible	Do the right things
Tell people what to do and how to do it	Share the Why and Empower your teams
Protect you by securing everyone's buy-in	Work with the right stakeholders and move on with speed
Go through extensive and lengthy review processes	Work with the right stakeholders and move on with speed
Command & Control	Trust and leverage people's own inner leadership and insight
Keep information to your chest	Free the flow of information. Share and support as much as you can
Decision pushed to the top	Tap into the team's collective intelligence and define a more agile decision process
Hierarchies	Dynamic governance - Holacracy
Reaction driven	Creation

By putting a different kind of glasses (trust, instead of fear), one can start to embody a new kind of leadership.

Before we look in the next section at precisely the qualities we need to nurture as well as the benefits of trust-based leadership, I just could not resist to share this beautiful quote from Einstein. Another way to look at the limiting "filters" one needs to free himself from:

"A human being is part of the whole called by us universe, a part limited in time and space. We experience ourselves, our thoughts and feelings as something separate from the rest. A kind of optical delusion of consciousness. This delusion is a kind of prison for us, restricting us to our personal desires and to affection for a few persons nearest to us. Our task must be to free ourselves from the prison by widening our circle of compassion to embrace all living

creatures and the whole of nature in its beauty. The true value of a human being is determined by the measure and the sense in which they have obtained liberation from the self. We shall require a substantially new manner of thinking if humanity is to survive."

Characteristics of trust-based leadership

The truth is, it can be hard to change our patterns and eventually our behaviors. Since we have been "moulded" for so many years to act defensively at work, to protect ourselves and our teams, it may not always be easy to embrace a trust-based perspective.

"So, what does it look like to be driven, not by fear, but by a higher purpose, a sense of wholeness, our soul?"
This is the question Frederic Laloux asks in his book "Reinventing Organizations" as he talks about fear-based leadership. And then describes how it would look like not to be driven by fear:

"What replaces fear? A capacity to trust the abundance of life. All wisdom traditions posit the profound truth that there are two fundamental ways to live life: from fear and scarcity or from trust and abundance. In Evolutionary-Teal, we cross the chasm and learn to decrease our need to control people and events. We come to believe that even if something unexpected happens or if we make mistakes, things will turn out all right, and when they don't, life will have given us an opportunity to learn and grow"

"If all you have known in your professional life are workplaces where politics and conflicts were the rule, it may be nearly impossible to consider that something else can exist. And that has to do with our worldview (...). Do we see the world as a place of dangers where we are better off protecting ourselves from external (perceived) risks (.i.e separation) or a place where we can take bold steps towards authenticity, vulnerability, trust and wholeness ?"

So, what happens when you stop being driven by fear. What is then emerging instead?
I can see a few things unfolding when we are able to change our "glasses" through which we see others and the world.

You attract like-minded people, and become a "magnet".

Some might call it attraction or resonance.
Because trust/collaboration/respect/empathy/wholeness is how you see the world, how you look at situations in which you get engaged, you naturally see the good in others, you see and appreciate their potential. It is not about being naïve or helpless. It is just about being, without putting a mask, and see the human being in others.

You in turn free other, let them express their own wholeness

Because others see that you are free, and not driven by your ego or your own personal agenda, that gives them the permission to become that too. This is to me a very important aspect. Have you ever had a leader in your own organization having an impact just by expressing himself authentically, empathically, with humility and yet with power? How liberating and inspiring!

You accept and enjoy people difference.

Others feel seen and heard. You collaborate, you are equals. Yes, roles might be different, but you are not on a pedestal nor put others on a pedestal either. You end up acknowledging and leveraging those differences, people's unique strengths and abilities. Their unique brilliance.

How Conflict can be Healthy

For many years, I really believed that conflict equaled anger, and that anger led to conflict. I could see myself occasionally avoiding conflict, mostly because I did not know how to deal with it. I just did not have the skills to properly address conflict and manage anger, mine and others.

But it does not have to be always like that. As a matter of fact, conflict is sometimes inevitable, and can be healthy.

For instance, the company Morning Star says that "conflict avoidance remains their major organizational issue and that making that first move to confront someone is hard".

But when trust permeates the corporate fabric, conflict can be resolved in ways that leave people less emotionally affected. I would argue that the ability (or inability) of a company to deal with conflict is also a great indicator of its fabric's health.

Without conflict, we can be over-accommodating or over-protective, and in both cases, we stop being true to ourselves when interacting with colleagues. And because being true to ourselves is at the heart of any trust-based fabric, it is critical that conflict is to be addressed. Precisely because employees are encouraged to « sense and respond » and take initiative when they sense this is the right thing to do, they will "fight" for what they believe is the right thing. But they will "fight" for what they believe should be done if they know that they operate in a trust-based environment.

Conflict is inevitable and people will disagree in the workplace. But when a culture of empathy has been nurtured, and nonviolent communication has been taught and practiced, we can start to

a. Hear and accept the view of the other
b. Differentiate between our thoughts and behaviors
c. Mindfully respond to conflict and disagreement

Mindfulness practices should be learned and practiced as they lead to much healthier corporate fabrics. Becoming more aware of how we see the world, how we respond to the perceived reality of the situations we encounter is certainly not always easy, but can become healthy if companies encourage mindful conflict resolution.

Let's have a deeper look at this very important aspect as it is a key ingredient of the trust-based leadership and environment leaders should seek to foster.

Mindful interactions in the workplace

As we move from the intrapersonal to the interpersonal, and to personal leadership, taking into account someone else's world, and the place where their world and ours meet is important.

This means recognizing that the other person has his own perceptions, feelings and needs, which we can likely perceive as different from ours, especially in times of conflict or disagreement. This is really about developing more mindful interactions with our colleagues

What does it means to be mindful in our interactions with others, for instance coworkers?

We discussed earlier Non Violent Communication, which in essence is about arriving at a mutual desire to give from the heart, by focusing the light of consciousness on four areas:

1. First, we observe what the others are saying or doing that is either enriching or not enriching our life. The challenge here is to be able to articulate this observation without introducing any judgment or evaluation.

2. Next, we state how we feel when we observe this action: are we hurt, scared, joyful, amused, irritated?

3. And thirdly, we say what needs of ours are connected to the feelings we have identified. An awareness of these three components is present when we use NVC to clearly and honestly express how we are.

4. Followed immediately with the fourth component – a very specific request. This fourth component addresses what we are wanting from the other person that would enrich our lives or make life more wonderful for us.

Thus, part of NVC is to express these four pieces of information very clearly, verbally or by other means. The other part of this communication consists of receiving the same four pieces of information from others. We connect with them by first sensing what they are observing, feeling and needing; then we discover what would enrich their lives by receiving the fourth piece — their request.

The essence of NVC is in our consciousness of the four components, not in the actual words that are exchanged. If you think about it, every single step of the process requires us to be aware and mindful of others as well as ourselves. It is a moment-by-moment awareness, both of our external environment and our internal state.

And at work, I have always found that to be particularly challenging. The busyness and stress of our work lives make it really hard to cultivate that moment-to-moment awareness. And because sometimes so much is asked of us, we tend to focus more on ourselves and less on the needs of other people as a result.

This was famously demonstrated in the classic Good Samaritan experiments conducted by John Darley and Daniel Batson in the 1970s. Darley and Batson assigned seminary students at Princeton University to deliver a talk on the Good Samaritan. While on their way to their presentation, the students passed someone (working with the researchers) who was slumped over and groaning. The researchers tested all kinds of variables to see what might make the students stop to help, but only one variable mattered: whether or not the students were late for their talk. Only 10 percent of the students stopped to help when they were late; more than six times as many helped when they were not in a hurry.

This study suggests that people are not inherently morally insensitive, but when we are stressed, scared, hurried, it is easy to lose touch with our deepest values. By helping us stay attuned to what is happening around us in the present moment, regardless of the time, mindfulness helps us stay connected to what is most important.

And then ... performance

Now, as we close this chapter on personal leadership, you may wonder: ok, great leaders, are they not about driving exceptional results ? Fantastic returns to shareholders? Market share gains? Reinventing companies? Leading change?

Yes, of course, they are !

As a matter of fact, I started this chapter by saying that leadership really comes down to a few key attributes:

1. Leaders get things down and get results
2. Leaders are agents of change
3. By inspiring with authenticity and trust

Change will happen, and things will get done. But for change and performance to be sustained, heart-based and trust-based leadership need to permeate the company's fabric.

Great results may temporarily help to foster a positive "climate", but when more difficult times occur, the lack of leadership, from "formal" leaders and from anyone, really, will be exposed.

Individuals will fall back to fear-based defensive mechanisms. For the fabric to truly deliver sustainable performance, it has to be inherently resilient. And resilience is created by the kind of leadership we discussed in this chapter.

Not only resilience, but what companies are all seeking today in this more and more changing, dynamic and digital world we live in : innovation !

Chapter 8
Innovation Unleashed

Speed, Agility and Innovation

The true story behind the invention of the chess board has been lost in time.

"The story is often told in the form of an humble servant, a mathematician, showing his creation with the Chinese emperor. The emperor was so impressed he offered the inventor a reward of his choosing.

The mathematician, asked that one grain of rice be placed on the first square of the board and that he be doubled on each subsequent square. The emperor, impressed by the inventor's apparent modesty, protests, believing that the reward is too small – but the mathematician persists.

When they reach the 32nd square, the reward amounts to the production from a small field- significant but not unreasonable. But the emperor could still remain an emperor. And the inventor could still retain his head. Yet, by the 64th square, it is estimated that the total amount of rice would amount to a pile the size of Mount Everest, or would cover entirely the surface of the Earth. Of course, the emperor could not honor such a request. In some versions of the story, once he realizes that he's been tricked, he has the inventor beheaded. But that is another story …"

The second half of the chessboard is a phrase coined by Ray Kurzweil an American author, inventor, futurist, and a director of engineering at Google. The key point being that once you reach the second half of the chessboard, changes are exponential. The story behind the chess board is a tale about exponential growth and accelerated change.

Things that were only a dream a short 10 years ago are now possible: driverless car for instance, or artificial intelligence. In other words, in many technological areas, we are today entering the second half of the chessboard.

I have been working in IT for more than 2 decades and meeting with organizations' Heads of Information Technology

(CTO, CIO…) on a constant basis. What they often would tell me is how much they feel overwhelmed by this "acceleration" . The business world is becoming more competitive, and for companies to thrive, they need speed and agility. Speed of innovation, of getting products and services faster to market, of designing and implementing new business models.

And for the IT departments, they will need the agility expected by their own business units (their internal customers) to deliver on the required agile IT services.

Interestingly, and more recently, I have started to witness how those companies are getting more and more aware of the need to match it with organizational agility. Something, they will admit, had been completely overlooked in the past, but now is making its way on their agenda.

In particular, in our modern age, where businesses need to take decisions faster and faster. This "acceleration" increasingly creates (unbearable ?) tension within organizations, which people find it more and more difficult to deal with. Some might even get "lost" with that new level of complexity and pace of change.

The human machine cannot be stretched infinitely. Similarly, organizations need to evolve to better "sense and respond" what is the best next move. They are more likely to innovate and thrive when they unleash the potential of individuals and the power of self-organizing team.

In addition, it is widely accepted that innovation happens more and more at the edge of the company, not at its core. While large corporations have massive R&D resources, and some of the brightest minds of their industry, they will often lack the culture of exploration and risk taking required for innovation. The layers found in typical hierarchical structures distance the executives at the top from market signals and emerging trends and adjacent innovations. Startup and innovation will be formed at the periphery of global large organizations, and therefore corporations increasingly need to foster a culture that can quickly sense and address the energy developing at the edge.

As we saw earlier, Holacracy integrates 2 important concepts:

- "Sense and respond" vs "Predict and control"
- "Processing tension", tension being defined as « the felt-sense of a specific gap between current reality and a sensed potential"

Therefore, innovation can emerge when an environment in which people are encouraged to sense issues and/or opportunities is created, and when people feel empowered to do something about those tensions. Providing more autonomy as well as role clarity and accountability will go a long way and is critical for people to feel they need and can address tensions once identified.

As Frederic Laloux writes:

> *"In a self-managing organization, change can come from any person who senses that change is needed. This is how nature has worked for millions of years. Innovation doesn't happen centrally, according to plan, but at the edges, all the time, when some organism senses a change in the environment and experiments to find an appropriate response. Some attempts fail to catch on; others rapidly spread to all corners of the ecosystem"*

Agile organizations, by design, provide the right structure for how companies will need to innovate in the future. While many companies are still looking for the magic formula to generate a constant flow of innovations to their business, and seek to develop the right processes and tools, one could argue that innovation can be both an art and science. You cannot always predict how and when your next innovation will take form, and therefore, companies can only seek to provide the most fertile ground for innovations to flourish.

The fertile ground for innovation

The benefits of dynamic governance are multiple. It provides the right operating system to

- Foster creativity and problem solving throughout the organization
- Facilitate and accelerate adaptation to change
- Engage and utilizes the energy of every member of the organization
- Generate high quality products and services
- Increase staff commitment to and identification with the organization
- Result in fewer, more satisfying meetings
- Decrease the odds of burnout
- Develop self-discipline
- Support leadership among peers

As Frederic Laloux writes in Reinventing Organizations,

"Strategy happens organically, all the time, everywhere, as people toy with ideas and test them out in the field. The organization evolves, morphs, expands, or contracts, in response to a process of collective intelligence. Reality is the great referee, not the CEO, the board or a committee. What works gathers momentum and energy within the organization; other ideas fail to catch on and wither"

Because we become more empowered human beings, as opposed to servile team members of hierarchies, dynamic governance models, like Holacracy, provide the right foundation for innovation to emerge.

Let me take a very pragmatic example of how innovation often gets stalled, and how a more agile model will instead "release" the flow of information and innovation.

In Holacracy, there are specific meetings whose sole objective is to process tensions. People would bring their tension to a meeting, hoping to make a change and improve the situation. The words have barely gotten out of your mouth when one of your colleagues jumps in. "Yeah, I agree that X doesn't work. But you know what? Y doesn't work either!" Before you know it, everyone has added their own tensions to the table, and your attempts to create change in a specific area are stalled. Holacracy's meetings are designed to avoid this frustratingly common situation. They protect the space for one person to bring up a tension, propose a solution, and actually initiate meaningful change with everyone's contribution. In order to do this, the meeting processes do not allow other people to simply pile their own reactions and related issues on top. Providing that space for individuals to safely and confidently express their proposal increases the chance of innovation to truly happen.

144

In addition, Holacracy is designed specifically to harness and honor what makes us so human, our creativity. Too often, in organizations, we experience great frustration because we can sense tensions but we don't have the capacity to turn them into creative improvements. When an organization is running on Holacracy, everyone is empowered to process their tensions. Human creativity and ingenuity becomes the company's most valued tool — not just for coming up with new products or services but for continually improving the way people work together and organize. The result is a much more deeply fulfilling experience of being a creative partner rather than a cog in the system.

Too many organizations adopt a parent-child relationship to their employees. Modern management hierarchies almost inevitably treat people like children, who need to be supervised, told what to do, and taken care of. Holacracy doesn't treat people as subordinate, or needing to be managed, motivated, or mothered. It treats them as mature enough to manage their own workflows, lead their own roles, and seek the help and resources they need to do so. It honors each person's sovereignty, seeing them as perfectly capable of managing themselves, driving their projects, staying motivated, and taking care of their own needs. In other words, it treats them as adults. And as adult, they will feel empowered to be creative and innovate.

You cannot always predict how and when your next innovation will take form, and therefore, companies can only seek to provide the most fertile ground for innovations to flourish. Having the right organization is one way to do it. Another way, as we discussed, is to ensure that people in your organization can feel totally empowered to innovate. When everyone gets clearer about his needs/potential/roles, in an enabling organization, creativity and innovation will freely emerge.

In the book "How will you measure your life", authors James Allworth, Karen Dillon and Clayton Christensen share the story of Honda's unanticipated way of succeeding in the US market. Unanticipated, because they ended up being successful through the smaller Super Cub motorbike after they had elaborated their original strategy around bigger motorbikes and competing head-to-head against American incumbents.

They noted the following:

"Honda's experience in building a new motorcycle business in America highlights the process by which every strategy is formulated and subsequently evolves. As Professor Henry Mintzberg taught, options for your strategy spring from two very different sources. The first source is anticipated opportunities—the opportunities that you can see and choose to pursue.

In Honda's case, it was the big-bike market in the United States. When you put in place a plan focused on these anticipated opportunities, you are pursuing a deliberate strategy. The second source of options is unanticipated—usually a cocktail of problems and opportunities that emerges while you are trying to implement the deliberate plan or strategy that you have decided upon. At Honda, what was unanticipated were the problems with the big bikes, the costs associated with fixing them, and the opportunity to sell the little Super Cub motorbikes.

The decision sometimes is an explicit decision; often, however, a modified strategy coalesces from myriad day-to-day decisions to pursue unanticipated opportunities and resolve unanticipated problems. When strategy forms in this way, it is known as emergent strategy. "

I mentioned that story because a few things needed to happen for Honda to capture that piece of the market and succeed on their new emergent strategy. They needed

     1. to sense the opportunity (the book goes in more details about how this happened)

     2. to swiftly abandon the anticipated strategy and execute on the emergent strategy quickly

Both can be achieved with greater chances of success if your organization has what it takes to embrace the emergent new strategy. This will never be science, and more of an art, but you can respond more decisively when your organization has embraced the kind of agile fabric we have discuss above.

     In addition to agility and empowerment, self-awareness and mindfulness are what you really want to develop in your teams. While you want to create an atmosphere where people can drive for success, it really depends how you approach it. If they are stressed, or burned-out, they certainly will not be available to innovate and create. Neuroscience has shown that, in order to be productive, one needs to be present and fully available. People do not need more adrenaline, but instead need to have a more idle and peaceful mind. Today, because of the craziness of our lives at work, it sometimes feel as we were in an energy crisis! Our own energy!

Innovation happens when both the personal and organizational soil is fertile. All it takes is to challenge the status-quo and take bold steps towards the workplace we envision for us all, places of growth, creativity, expansion and innovation.

Chapter 9
Purpose

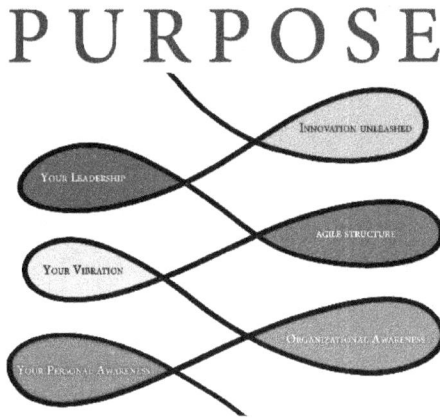

So, now that we looked at this ascending journey towards performance, leadership and innovation, one might ask : "So what?". Is this about reaching our full potential at work? Our leadership capabilities? Expressing our very best?

Well, yes ... but not only!

Yes, aiming at becoming the most vibrant agents of our next generation corporate fabrics is in itself a transformational journey and a new paradigm. And one that not just leaders and managers, but all of us, should really be looking at embracing.

But I think there is a more to it. If we indeed consider the dynamic at our workplace as an "ascension" opportunity, one in which we have the chance to transform ourselves as well as our organizations, I can see the need for this "ascending energy" to be guided and directed.

The same way, for instance, our thoughts and actions need to be directed by our intention and will, the energy we spend at work, both to bring value to our companies and to develop, not just the business, but ourselves too, needs to be directed. But by what? And towards what? Some might say that the answer is obvious: "it should be directed by and towards the profit our companies need to make"!

I would like here to give it a different perspective. I think it instead should be guided by purpose. Our individual purpose and our collective purpose. And once purpose becomes the driving force behind the "ascension" we have discussed in this book, profit will flow, as a natural consequence.

Being guided by purpose

The research is clear - employee engagement has a huge impact on organizational performance. Benefits are huge (Service, Sales, Quality, Safety, Retention, Sales, Profit and Total Shareholder Returns among others as shown in many studies around the world that show a correlation between employee engagement and those benefits).

But the average organization has today only 1 in 4 of their employees who are engaged. The rest, about 75% of their organization, are doing just what they have to do to get by, or worse.

Jack Welch once said that the three most important things that an organization should be measuring about its performance are cash flow, customer satisfaction, and employee engagement.

How then, do we develop engagements in our organizations?

Daniel H. Pink, in his book «Drive», shows how «carrot & stick» (extrinsic drivers) approaches do not work to sustainably motivate people (as we had believed for many years) in today's new kind of jobs. Our current business operating system–which is built around external, carrot-and-stick motivators–doesn't work and often does harm. We need an upgrade. Science has now shown us that we need:

1. *Autonomy* – the desire to direct our own lives.
2. *Mastery* — the urge to get better and better at something that matters.
3. *Purpose* — the yearning to do what we do in the service of something larger than ourselves.

The secret to high performance and satisfaction—at work, at school, and at home—is the deeply human need to direct our own lives, to learn and create new things, and to do better for our world and ourselves.

Developing purpose and meaning, of all three factors identified by Daniel Pink, is what managers seem to be the least comfortable with and for which they appear to be the least skilled. And yet, this might be the most powerful of all three.

As a coach, I have seen magic happening once individuals are aligned with their purpose. Instead of coaching people on how to address or fix limiting behaviors, it can be far more effective to help them connect with their values, purpose and identity.

In the same vein, in their great book "How will you measure your life", authors James Allworth, Karen Dillon and Clayton Christensen discussed two theories which have been debated, and still are, for decades. Jensen and Meckling's and Hertzberg's.

"Many managers have adopted Jensen and Meckling's underlying thinking—believing that when you need to convince others that they should do one thing and not another, you just need to pay them to do what you want them to do, when you want them to do it. It's easy, it's measurable; in essence, you are able to simply delegate management to a formula. Even parents can default to thinking that external rewards are the most effective way to motivate the behavior they want from their children—for example, offering their children a financial reward as an incentive for every A on a report card. (...)

The problem with incentives theory is that there are powerful anomalies that it cannot explain. For example, some of the hardest-working people on the planet are employed in nonprofits and charitable organizations. Some work in the most difficult conditions imaginable—disaster recovery zones, countries gripped by famine and flood. They earn a fraction of what they would if they were in the private sector.

Well, there is a second school of thought—often called two-factor theory, or motivation theory—that turns the incentive theory on its head. It acknowledges that you can pay people to want what you want—over and over again. But incentives are not the same as motivation. True motivation is getting people to do something because they want to do it. This type of motivation continues, in good times and in bad. (...)

Herzberg's (...) theory distinguishes between two different types of factors: hygiene factors and motivation factors. On one side of the equation, there are the elements of work that, if not done right, will cause us to be dissatisfied. These are called hygiene factors. Hygiene factors are things like status, compensation, job security, work conditions, company policies, and supervisory practices. It matters, for example, that you don't have a manager who manipulates you for his own purposes—or who doesn't hold you accountable for things over which you don't have responsibility. Bad hygiene causes dissatisfaction. You have to address and fix bad hygiene to ensure that you are not dissatisfied in your work.

Compensation is a hygiene factor. You need to get it right. But all you can aspire to is that employees will not be mad at each other and the company because of compensation. (...)

This is an important insight from Herzberg's research: if you instantly improve the hygiene factors of your job, you're not going to suddenly love it. At best, you just won't hate it anymore. The opposite of job dissatisfaction isn't job satisfaction, but rather an absence of job dissatisfaction. They're not the same thing at all."

And this is really where purpose becomes so important. Be it individual or company-wide.

James Allworth, Karen Dillon and Clayton Christensen further asked:

" So, what are the things that will truly, deeply satisfy us, the factors that will cause us to love our jobs? These are what Herzberg's research calls motivators. Motivation factors include challenging work, recognition, responsibility, and personal growth. Feelings that you are making a meaningful contribution to work arise from intrinsic conditions of the work itself. Motivation is much less about external prodding or stimulation, and much more about what's inside of you, and inside of your work.

This, in turn, can mean they get paid well; careers that are filled with motivators are often correlated with financial rewards. But sometimes the reverse is true, too—financial rewards can be present without the motivators. In my assessment, it is frightfully easy for us to lose our sense of the difference between what brings money and what causes happiness. You must be careful not to confuse correlation with causality in assessing the happiness we can find in different jobs.

We should always remember that beyond a certain point, hygiene factors such as money, status, compensation, and job security are much more a by-product of being happy with a job rather than the cause of it. Realizing this frees us to focus on the things that really matter. "

Which leads me to the most simple, yet the most inspirational leadership story I have ever come across.

Build your cathedral

This is the story of the three stone cutters:

«*One day a traveller, walking along a lane, came across 3 stonecutters working in a quarry. Each was busy cutting a block of stone. Interested to find out what they were working on, he asked the first stonecutter what he was doing. "I am cutting a stone!"*

Still no wiser the traveller turned to the second stonecutter and asked him what he was doing. "I am cutting this block of stone to make sure that it's square, and its dimensions are uniform, so that it will fit exactly in its place in a wall."

A bit closer to finding out what the stonecutters were working on but still unclear, the traveller turned to the third stonecutter. He seemed to be the happiest of the three and when asked what he was doing replied: "I am building a cathedral."

154

This speaks about leadership and purpose. It is important for each individual to understand the cathedral he (or she) is building as well as his role (alignment, strategic role) in the building of the cathedral. In today's corporate worlds, it is easy to keep busy! Our «To Do» lists never really stop to grow. Therefore, keeping that strategic direction is critical. Being busy is not (and will not be) the best criteria to evaluate how people do. Instead, organizations will instead start to look more at how people are able to cope with complexity, prioritize things while making strategic choices.

Ultimately, the stone cutters story is about purpose and joy. Knowing its contribution to the bigger picture keeps us joyful, engaged and motivated. Contributing to others and having a strong sense of purpose are two of the most important needs every human being strives to fulfill. And in our jobs, our level of performance will increased as a result.

The day we are clear on the cathedral we are here to build, nothing can stop us. Call it life purpose, personal mission or vision. Once aligned with our purpose, actions take place, joy support us effortlessly and others get inspired too in the process! It is about developing a higher vision for our lives, our work and our roles as individual contributors, managers and leaders. More than ever, leaders have also the chance to look at their job as unique opportunities to develop the best version possible of them and their team members, and develop a renewed sense of purpose at work. Asking yourself the question «what is the cathedral I want to build and I want my team to build» is a great start.

Let me know expand further on the importance of purpose and alignment. The Logical (or Neurological) levels framework is one of the most powerful "tools" I have used over the years.

Logical Levels

From the work of Gregory Bateson, Robert Dilts, a Californian psychologist, has built an elegant model for thinking about personal change, learning and communication that brings together ideas of context, levels of learning, and perceptual positions. Logical levels form an internal hierarchy in which each level is progressively more psychologically encompassing and powerful. Logical levels separate the action from the person's identity. A person is not defined by his behaviors or his skills.

In the way our brain works, there are natural hierarchies or levels of experience. For instance, people speak of responding to things on different 'levels'. Someone might say that an experience was negative on one level, but positive on another level. People intuitively have a feel for these internal hierarchies.

Gregory Bateson first developed the logical levels system as a way to describe human ideas for forming projected actions, pointing out that in the processes of learning, change, and communication, there were natural hierarchies of classification. The function of each level is to organize the information on the level below it, and the rules for changing something on one level were different from those for changing something on a lower level. Changing something on a lower level could affect the upper levels; however changing something in the upper levels would necessarily change things on the lower levels, in order to support the higher level change. Bateson noted that it was the confusion between thinking on different logical levels that often created problems for people.

Robert Dilts followed Gregory Bateson's work (1991). He originally provided a clear and succinct description of the structure, nature, and workings of logical levels regarding our key conversations in developing goals and results. He considered that, in working with project development, the following levels seem to be the most basic and the most important to consider:

1. Who I am. Identity.
2. Values. What's important and why? Includes world-view, categories, comparative values.
3. Capabilities. My capabilities. States, strategies, and meta-programs.
4. Do. What I do, or have done. Specific behaviors and actions.
5. Environment. The external context.

Neurological Levels

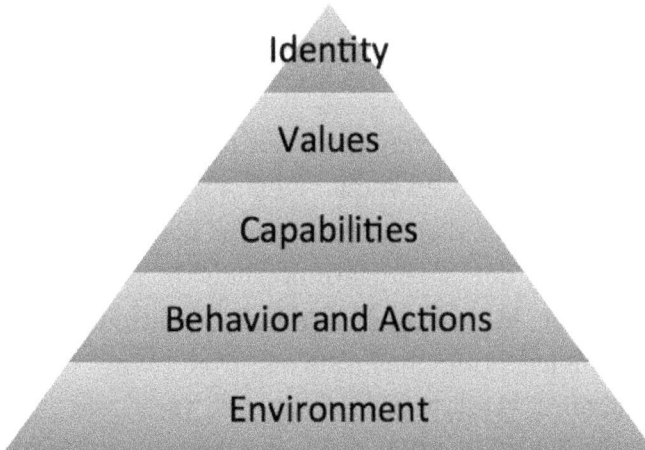

Identity

Values

Capabilities

Behavior and Actions

Environment

In other words, instead of addressing an employee's problematic actions or behaviors (the second level on the picture), a manager could instead work on levels above. He could work on understanding the new skills and capabilities that this employee would need to acquire. But he could also help that person to become more aligned with his values, and even more powerfully, with his identity and even his purpose (above identity, not represented above)

Once someone changes at one level, all levels down are positively affected. And changed in a sustainable way.

Consequently, working on a team's (or a person's) values, identity or vision will align all levels below and result into higher engagement and performance.

Start with Why

Similarly, I would like to mention the well-known work of Simon Sinek "Start with Why"[19] . It is linked to some extent to the concepts of logical levels. What Simon Sinek says is that:

- All people and organizations know "What" they do
- Some know "How" they do it (through differentiating value proposition, proprietary processes or Unique Selling Points)
- Very few companies know "Why" they do what they do. The "Why" is about their purpose, cause, and their belief, in other words, why does an organization exist in the first place?
- All great leaders and inspired organizations think, act, communicate from the inside out, from "Why" over "How" to "What".
- People don't buy "What" you do; they buy "Why" you do it. "What" you do simply serves as proof of what you believe.

---

[19] http://www.startwithwhy.com/

- And the goal is not to make business with people who need "What" you have, the goal is to make business with people who believe what you believe.

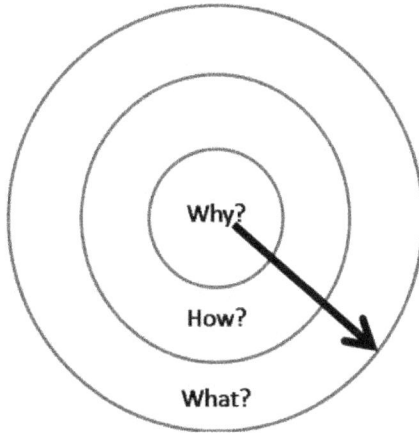

He further illustrates his point looking at how Apple does exactly that: selling the "Why" to their customers. He imagines how Apple's marketing message starting with the "What" would look like. Apple would say: "We make great computers. They are beautifully designed, simple to use. Do you want to buy one?" . Chances are that few people would feel inspired by that. It does say what they do and how they are better in a typical marketing strategy. But Apple starts with their "Why" and say - "In everything we do, we believe in challenging the status quo and thinking differently. We do this by making our products beautifully designed and simple to use. We just happen to make great computers. Do you want to buy one?"

Similarly, for any teams (and even individuals), as discussed in the cathedral story, it is critical to start with the "Why". The "Why" will create engagement, momentum, alignment and ... results.

Purpose should really be permeating our corporate fabrics. It could be our individual purpose as well as our companies' collective purpose. The fabric we have discussed, ascending upwards, will bring and exceed the anticipated results and performance of all of its stakeholders are infused by a sense of purpose.

One might find it difficult at first to believe that a company mission and purpose could indeed be our ultimate compass. But what if indeed we could turn it upside down? Think purpose and mission first!

Dr Viktor Frankl says it so beautifully in his book "Man's Search for Meaning". In his famous book, he tells the story of how he survived the Holocaust by finding personal meaning in the experience, which gave him the will to live through it.

And he says : "Success, like happiness, cannot be pursued; it must ensue, and it only does so as the unintended side-effect of one's personal dedication to a cause greater than oneself."

Translate that to our corporate world, this is also saying that by focusing on purpose rather than profits, profits will come, as a natural consequence.

Profits

So, what we are really saying is that each employee, energized by his own purpose, can embrace and energized in turn the overall company's purpose. Yes, a company's purpose provides direction. But in addition, each employee, aligned with his own vision and purpose, will propel the company's purpose even further. And this will lead to higher profits!

In today's corporate world, profit and market share gains are what seems to be driving what we do, and guiding how we make decisions at work. Yet, as we have seen, the objective is purpose, not profit. Profit is like the air we breathe. We need air to live, but we do not live to breathe. Profits are a side-effect of people shining at work, guided by a personal and a collective purpose.

By focusing on purpose rather than profits, profits will be made more "naturally, as a by-product of everyone's acting as a living cell serving what the company is called for.

And when everyone in the company is indeed driven by purpose, everyone is all in! People will not turn sight if they see something not working for which they know there is a solution. With the purpose as a guiding light, everyone, individually and collectively, is empowered to sense what might be called for.

The new fabric I am envisioning for our modern workplaces is one in which we can all embody our fullest potential, clearer about, and aligned with, our purpose, while bringing an organization's deeper purpose to life. It is a virtuous circle and not a dichotomy: when we are at our best, we do serve the company's very purpose. And as it unfolds, we are in turn nourished and fulfilled, and inspired to give our best at work. Our most creative, engaged, collaborative and driven self is brought forward. And profits are made, in a sustainable and ecological way.

Closing Note

As you close the last chapter of this book, I have only one hope.

It is that you will feel even more compelled to make your own workplace more engaged by embracing the type of corporate fabric we have discussed.

As Gandhi once said: "Be the change that you wish to see in the world".

If we wish to make our workplace a better, more creative and purposeful place for the people we have the chance to work and interact with, and be a powerful change agent, start somewhere, anywhere. Small, big, it does not matter.

Imagine what it would be like if managers, leaders, and team members alike, could all develop more authenticity in their relationships with their colleagues? And step up to their full leadership potential.

Through more ecological connections, empowered and liberated organizations, purpose and bringing their whole self at work.

Oh, and by the way, while still meeting their sales and productivity numbers ... and fostering a culture of risk taking and innovation!

This is possible, and starts with each of us.

Thank you so much for the time you spent reading this book.

About the Author

Releasing my first book, "Ecological Leadership", back in 2013 was not something I had really planned!

Not until I started to become more aware of the huge opportunity we all have to transform our workplace. It then became something I really felt I had to do, an urge to share about what was becoming so alive within me.

I started some 25 years ago in the Information Technology industry, and have held several management and leadership positions while graduating from an Executive MBA in France.

In addition, I trained myself in Nonviolent Communication and Nonviolent Communication at work. And later became a Professional Coach as well as a Certified Holacracy Practitioner. I also studied various Personal Development practices, Neuro-Linguistic Programming (NLP), Transactional analysis, Meditation, Mindfulness, Eastern philosophies…

That journey started to unveil in me two very important things: my core values and purpose. I came to realize how much our self-limiting beliefs and patterns, personal self-sabotage strategies and high tyrannical expectations tend to separate ourselves further from our full potential.

The resulting lack of personal empowerment sadly creates several collateral damages in our lives. At work, this can result into:

- Unauthentic relationships
- Strategies and responses developed in autopilot mode
- Low engagement
- Stifled creativity

- Unchallenged status-quo
- Untapped potential
- Insufficient innovation

Throughout this book, and other material available on my website, I seek to share what I know is possible for us all so that we can transform ourselves and our workplaces.

*****

Note: if you would like to comment or share on what we have discussed in this book, please do so at : www.ericmarin.fr/blog[20]

---

[20] https://www.ericmarin.fr/blog

www.ingramcontent.com/pod-product-compliance
Lightning Source LLC
Chambersburg PA
CBHW060030210326
41520CB00009B/1071